# DE-DOLLARIZATION

ISBN 978-1-686479-59-5 (Paperback)

Copyright © 2019 Gal Luft and Anne Korin

All rights reserved.

No part of this publication may be reproduced, distributed, or transmitted in any form or by any means, including photocopying, recording, or other electronic or mechanical methods, without the prior written permission of the publisher, except in the case of brief quotations embodied in critical reviews and certain other noncommercial uses permitted by copyright law.

# DE-DOLLARIZATION

*The revolt against the dollar and the rise of a new financial world order*

GAL LUFT AND ANNE KORIN

*The best way to destroy the capitalist
system is to debauch the currency.*
Lenin

# CONTENTS

List of acronyms .................................................................... ix
Prologue ............................................................................. xiii
Introduction: America First and the rise of the rest ...................... xix

Chapter 1: Weaponizing currency ................................................. 1
Chapter 2: The dollar busters ..................................................... 21
Chapter 3: Is red the new green? ................................................. 39
Chapter 4: As good as gold: From petrodollar to petroyuan ........ 63
Chapter 5: Another BRICS in the wall ....................................... 82
Chapter 6: Rising phoenix ....................................................... 100
Chapter 7: Alice in Wonderland economics .............................. 121
Chapter 8: Toward a currency protection strategy .................... 145

Epilogue ............................................................................. 169
About the authors ................................................................ 173
Endnotes ............................................................................ 175

# LIST OF ACRONYMS

| | |
|---|---|
| ADNOC | Abu Dhabi's National Oil Company |
| AfCFTA | African Continental Free Trade Agreement |
| AIIB | Asian Infrastructure Investment Bank |
| ASEAN | Association for South East Asian Nations |
| BRI | Belt and Road Initiative |
| BRICS | Brazil, Russia, India, China, and South Africa |
| CBDC | Central Bank Digital Currency |
| CNOOC | China National Offshore Oil Corporation |
| CNPC | China National Petroleum Corporation |
| CPEC | China-Pakistan Economic Corridor |
| CRFB | Committee for a Responsible Federal Budget |
| CRS | Common Reporting Standard |
| CPC | Communist Party of China |
| CBO | Congressional Budget Office |
| CRA | Contingent Reserve Arrangement |
| COMECON | Council for Mutual Economic Assistance |
| CAATSA | Countering America's Adversaries through Sanctions Act |
| CIPS | Cross-border Inter-bank Payments System |
| COFER | Currency Composition of Official Foreign Exchange Reserves |
| DCRI | Digital Currency Research Institute |
| DLT | Distributed Ledger Technology |
| EAEU | Eurasian Economic Union |

| | |
|---|---|
| ECB | European Central Bank |
| FAANG | Facebook, Amazon, Apple, Netflix, Google |
| FATCA | Foreign Account Tax Compliance Act |
| FCPA | Foreign Corrupt Practices Act |
| FRB | Fractional Reserve Banking |
| FOIP | Free and Open Indo-Pacific Strategy |
| FTA | Free Trade Agreement |
| GATT | General Agreement on Tariffs and Trade |
| GDP | Gross Domestic Product |
| GNP | Gross National Product |
| GCC | Gulf Cooperation Council |
| ICO | Initial Coin Offering |
| IBEC | International Bank for Economic Cooperation |
| IEEPA | International Emergency Economic Powers Act |
| IMF | International Monetary Fund |
| INF | Intermediate-range Nuclear Forces |
| INSTEX | Instrument in Support of Trade Exchanges |
| JCPOA | Joint Comprehensive Plan of Action |
| LNG | Liquefied Natural Gas |
| Mercosur | Mercado Común del Sur |
| MMT | Modern Monetary Theory |
| NIC | National Intelligence Council |
| NOC | National Oil Companies |
| NYMEX | New York Mercantile Exchange |
| NOPEC | No Oil Producing and Exporting Cartels Act |
| OFAC | Office of Foreign Assets Control |
| OMB | Office of Management and Budget |
| OMO | Open Market Operations |
| OPEC | Organization of Petroleum Exporting Countries |
| OTC | Over the Counter |
| PAYGO | Pay As You GO |
| PBoC | People's Bank of China |

| | |
|---|---|
| PCE | Personal Consumption Expenditure |
| PGM | Platinum Group Metals |
| PEP | Politically Exposed Person |
| PPP | Purchasing Power Parity |
| QE | Quantitative Easing |
| SCO | Shanghai Cooperation Organization |
| SWIFT | Society for Worldwide Interbank Financial Telecommunication |
| SACU | South African Customs Union |
| SAARC | South Asian Association for Regional Cooperation |
| SDR | Special Drawing Rights |
| STFI | Special Trade and Finance Instrument |
| SDN | Specially Designated Nationals and Blocked Persons |
| S&P | Standard & Poor |
| SAFE | State Administration of Foreign Exchange |
| SOE | State Owned Enterprises |
| SPFS | System for Transfer of Financial Messages |
| TR | Transferable Ruble |
| TBAC | Treasury Borrowing Advisory Committee |
| UST | United States Treasuries |
| WTI | West Texas Intermediary |
| WTO | World Trade Organization |

# PROLOGUE

The question who will run the world in the 21st century would likely not have surfaced if not for a growing sense that the current superpower, the United States of America, is losing its mojo. While it is still the world's biggest economy, the strongest military power and the pillar of the rules-based international order, the United States is more divided, unfocused and indifferent to the world than at any other point since the Second World War. The fact that no great power—not even China—is capable of stepping into America's big shoes only adds to the sense of confusion. Time will tell if what we are experiencing today is a temporary funk or the beginning of Pax Americana's long goodbye and the transition to what Ian Bremmer and David Gordon have called a G-Zero world in which western influence is replaced by a vacuum and every nation is more or less for itself. The next few years will be America's opportunity to ensure the former is the answer. There is much to be done on multiple fronts. This book offers a glimpse into a strategic development that has received little notice in the U.S. domestic public conversation, yet if ignored could drive America's decline like no other. It has to do with our currency—for now, the world's currency—the U.S. dollar.

The dollar is the foundation of the U.S. economy and a key element of America's preeminence by virtue of its special status as the reserve currency of the world. The United States is home to less than five percent of the world's population and accounts for a fifth of world's GDP, yet 80 percent of international payments are made in its currency. This makes the dollar our national symbol and the world's most familiar brand. In one way or another we are all beholden to it. If the dollar were to lose its special status as the reserve currency of the world, the impact would be felt not only in our pocketbooks, our retirement plans, our healthcare costs, the value of our homes and our bank loans but also in America's ability to preserve its superpower status.

This is not a hypothetical scenario. In our increasingly chaotic world, the dollar is facing a challenge by a growing coalition of states and non-state actors who are fed up with what they believe to be America's overuse of sanctions and other coercive economic measures, its extraterritorial legal outreach and its treatment of the global financial system as its fiefdom. Through a variety of tactics, some stealth, others upfront, those actors seek to rewrite the rules of the 21$^{st}$ century and that includes challenging the dollar's hegemony over the world's monetary system. Their effort to undermine the dollar is intensifying by the day as more and more players jump on the bandwagon, moving their trades to non-dollar currencies and building mechanisms to circumvent the U.S. dominated financial system. It is only recently that the term "de-dollarization" has begun to appear in our public conversation, and like other new slow-moving threats, it has drawn mixed responses ranging from dismissal to alarm. Optimists view the effort to dethrone the dollar as yet another shenanigan by a group of tin-pot dictators whose primary interest is to evade sanctions, launder money, wreak havoc in the international system and further America's decline. The dollar system is robust, they claim, and the attacks on it are, at most, inconsequential pinpricks. Pessimists, on the other hand, see a violent storm gathering on the horizon. For them, America, crushed under a burden of unsustainable debt and extracting itself from the globalized system, is on a path of irreversible decline, and the fall of the dollar system is an inevitable manifestation of this decline.[1] This view is no longer held only by fringe economists but by some mainstream and highly respected financial institutions. For example, in July 2019, JP Morgan strategist Craig Cohen wrote in a note to investors: "We believe the dollar could lose its status as the world's dominant currency (which could see it depreciate over the medium term) due to structural reasons as well as cyclical impediments."[2]

It is not given to us to foresee who is correct. As is often the case in such debates, over the long run at some point each of the sides will be right, but then, as John Maynard Keynes said, in the long run we are all dead. As this book is being written, America's near-term economic indicators look fairly good. Equity markets are thriving, consumer confidence is high, unemployment has fallen to historically low levels, and the dollar is holding well against all the currencies that could potentially challenge it. More so, the instability in Europe has created uncertainty about the future of the euro, which is celebrating at the time of this writing its twentieth anniversary, and this could spell trouble for the world's second most widely traded currency. If the Eurozone were to break, this could buoy the dollar for quite some time. The other major currencies all have their problems and they are not performing much better. On its face, the dollar is unrivaled. But the surface-level calm and other countries' travails should not distract us from the deep-rooted problems the United States is facing. We are increasing our national debt at an unsustainable pace while the number of governments, institutions and individuals who reject America's international conduct and particularly its financial policing is growing by the day. Left unattended, the pushback against the dollar will gather more steam as more countries reclaim their sovereignty and opt to diversify their currency portfolios. And while each singular action may seem inconsequential, the cumulatively the efforts could ultimately cause death by a thousand cuts.

It would be imprudent to ignore the warning signs described in this book. On the other hand, panic is also unwarranted. The dollar is not likely to lose its special status tomorrow morning or next year. One should not underestimate the reputation, resilience and transparency of the American financial system, not to mention the strength of the dollar brand. What gives the dollar its strength is the faith in the stability and continuity of the American political system and America's uncontested military power. While many countries grumble about our conduct and some turn their backs on our rules-based order altogether, there are many more who still cherish the status quo authored by the United States almost a century ago and who are ready to fight for its preservation. Those fellow travelers should not be taken for granted.

The de-dollarization efforts of several countries described in the coming chapters are interesting, but in the grand scheme of things most of them bear little consequence for the United States. It is hard to see how a bunch of internationally isolated second and third-tier economies like Russia, Iran or Venezuela, even if working in concert, could topple the gigantic and widely accepted dollar system. But there is one country that can dramatically change this calculus - China. We would not have written this book if not for the historical transformation of U.S.-China relations unfolding right before our eyes. U.S. relations with China are presently at a critical junction. Forty years after the beginning of U.S.-China economic engagement, it is apparent that the relations are no longer complementary. The two countries, representing two diametrically opposed political, economic and social systems yet economically intertwined like conjoined twins, are locked in a trade war and a fierce struggle over $21^{st}$ century technology superiority. It is yet to be seen if China and the United States are headed toward an era of strategic adjustment in which a new path to coexistence is charted or if they are headed toward a full-blown Cold War 2.0 which could eventually decouple the two economies—if not worse. While both scenarios would add a great deal of instability to the world economy, the latter would have profound and multi-generational consequences for humanity. Should we end up in this direction, it can be assumed that China, a top holder of America's foreign debt, will spare no effort to de-dollarize not only its own economic system but that of its entire sphere of influence, if not the whole world. The new world order born out of a Cold War 2.0 would give rise to a China-Russia-led parallel financial universe which would compete with the dollar system, forcing all other nations, including some of America's closest allies, to make difficult choices.

To assess how serious of a risk de-dollarization poses to America's future both in the near term and the longer term we will explore the motives of each of the main players comprising what we call "the dollar insurgency." Listening to the viewpoints and grievances of policymakers, academics, bankers, and businesspeople in China, Russia, Europe, South Asia, Southeast Asia and the Middle East, has often made us cringe. Many of the complaints about the United States may not correspond with the way most Americans view themselves and their role in the world. But familiarity with the other side's thinking is critical for assessing the risk and crafting an effective response. Once we understand the insurgents' motives, we will cover the means they have at their disposal to advance their goal. In this, we will review their domestic monetary policies, their geo-economic rationale and their views about utilization of multinational organizations and financial mechanisms. We also describe attempts to utilize the global oil market as a lever by shifting more oil transactions from dollars to alternative currencies. We view the oil market as the dollar's first line of defense. If it succumbs to the de-dollarization movement, the rest of the multi-trillion dollar global commodity market will follow, draining hundreds of billions of dollars from the dollar circuit. We then move on to assess how the changes in technology, geopolitics and multinational organizations and corporations, including America's own Facebook, which recently announced the introduction of its own currency, are shaping a new monetary order for the 21$^{st}$ century and how America's economic hegemony would fare in that order, especially in light of socio-economic changes the United States itself is undergoing. We assess the long-term feasibility of some alternatives to the dollar, the role of gold and the potential impact of digital currencies based on distributed ledger technology (DLT), generically known as Blockchain. Understanding the potential of DLT - particularly in light of the rise of other complementing technologies like 5G, quantum computing, big data analytics and artificial intelligence - to change the global currency map is critical for the United States to stay ahead of its competitors. Finally, we offer some recommendations on how the United States can secure its economic hegemony so it can continue to lead for many years to come. Spoiler alert: none of the major solutions we offer are pain free. Most involve sacrifice and changes in national priorities which may not be palatable to our present day political class. But we hope that if Americans better understand the risks associated with continuing down the current path and realize that preserving the status of the dollar as reserve currency may be one of the biggest national security challenges of our time, they will be more open to do what it takes to shift the trajectory.

# INTRODUCTION: AMERICA FIRST AND THE RISE OF THE REST

> The dollar is our currency, but your problem.
> *U.S. Treasury Secretary John Connally to his European counterparts, 1971.*

When in the early 16$^{th}$ century the Czech nobleman Count of Schlick opened his mint in the small mountain town of Jáchymov in Bohemia (located in what is today the Czech Republic) he had no idea that six centuries later the name of the silver coin he created would become one of the world's most used words. The coin was originally referred to by its users as Schlicken thalers or Jáchymov's thalers, but its name was soon shortened to the German word taler which later became daler. By the middle of the century the term daler became a generic name for a variety of coins originating from Europe, and when in the early 1780s the founders of the new republic created across the Atlantic sought a name for their currency, they chose the descendent of the daler known today as the United States Dollar. Today the dollar is the world's most recognized brand and by far the most widely used currency. Roughly 1.5 trillion dollar worth of green 2.61 by 6.14 inches pieces of papers titled "Federal Reserve Note" change hands every year—most of the circulation taking place outside of the United States. It is not only the abundance of coins and bills that give the dollar its preeminence in the global economy but also the accumulation of other U.S. dollar denominated financial assets from commodities and real estate to equities and derivatives. More importantly, the reason the dollar is such a household name is its status as the reserve currency of the world.

## The hub that connects all spokes

A reserve currency is a national currency that is held by foreign countries in large quantities as protection against mishaps that can happen in their own economies. When central bankers consider which reserve currency to hold on their balance sheet, typically in the form of sovereign bonds, their first consideration is liquidity. They want to know that it would be easy to convert the bonds into cash when trouble arises, for example when they urgently need cash to defend their currency. They would therefore want to hold a significant part of their assets in highly trusted foreign currencies like dollars or euros. Countries also need dollar reserves to conduct their trade. When country A sells oil, food or manufactured goods to country B, it does not necessarily wish to receive country B's currency, which may be weak and volatile as is the case in many developing nations. It would prefer to settle the trade in a neutral and more reliable currency like the dollar. This simplifies the global currency exchange system. The late Stanford University professor Ronald McKinnon explained the convenience in using a central currency like the dollar: "With 150 national currencies in the world [if] you tried to trade each pair, there would be 11,175 foreign exchange markets! […] Thus, rather than trading all pairs of currencies bilaterally, in practice just one currency is chosen as the central vehicle currency. Then all trading and exchange takes place first against the vehicle currency before going to the others. By having all currency trading against that one currency […] we need to have just 149 foreign exchange markets—instead of 11,175."[1] One would expect that central currency to be issued by a country that is not only rich and strong but also commands trust and respect and projects stability. Hence the natural choice has been the dollar. The dollar is to the global monetary system what the English language is for human civilization—a hub that connects all spokes. In other words, the reason nations accumulate dollar reserves is that the U.S. economy is the dominant player in global trade and U.S. currency is reliable and totally convertible. No wonder the dollar makes up almost two thirds of all known central bank foreign exchange reserves with the other 150 currencies collectively comprising the rest. So widely received and trusted is the dollar that about half the countries of the world either peg their currencies to it or keep their currency within a defined trading range relative to it. This faith in the dollar has given America tremendous advantages over the years. With its currency always desired by others, the demand for dollar denominated Treasuries has grown more or less in sync with the expansion of the world economy. And because demand for dollars is always growing, the United States can issue more dollar denominated debt, knowing that there will always be takers. This has allowed consecutive U.S. administrations to borrow cheap money from the rest of the world and build America as the superpower that it is, but it has also allowed them to overspend and run the deficits that have inflated our $22 trillion and growing debt monster.

## The rise and fall of great currencies

The hegemony of the dollar over the global monetary system is the single most important source of America's power today—more so than its military. If not for the special status of the dollar, the United States would not be able to run the very same deficits that have enabled it to sustain the nearly one trillion dollar a year national defense complex which provides security not only to Americans but also to much of the rest of the world. For all the alarmism about the military challenges emanating from Russia and China, in today's military terms the United States is still the only superpower that can project significant military force to keep the peace in faraway places. But this can only last as long as our economy is strong, and the economy can only remain strong as long as the dollar retains its strategic status.

Historian Paul Kennedy demonstrated in his book *The Rise and Fall of the Great Powers* that imperial decline typically happens when an empire overstretches and can no longer afford to maintain its military power.[2] This means that if the dollar were to lose its preeminence, America's ability to defend itself and the free world would, too, erode. We should pay attention to the status of the dollar not only for its impact on our end-of-the-year bank statements but also because currency declines are a recurring symptom of great power declines. History has issued a very clear verdict on this. In the past six centuries, six currencies held global reserve status—the Portuguese escudo, the Spanish peso de ocho, the Dutch guilder, the French franc, the British pound and, most recently, the U.S. dollar. Each occupied the throne for roughly 80-100 years, corresponding with its country's international preeminence. In each one of the cases, when the empire began its decline, its currency lost its appeal as doubts began to creep about the empire's health and longevity. The erosion in the status of the currency denied the empire the ability to attract foreign investment and to borrow the money needed for it to keep up its imperial obligations. As money became scarcer and costlier to obtain, fewer resources were available for imperial upkeep, especially for the military that made imperial gains possible to begin with. Sensing the empire's decline, challengers began to rear their heads. This triggered fierce competition, arms race and wars. Beyond a certain point, with its currency losing much of its value, the empire could no longer handle the internal and external pressures, and it collapsed onto itself.

The greenback has been more or less at the helm since the 1920s, though its official coronation only took place during World War II. A century later, are we due for a change of guard? If so, can any single currency dethrone the dollar? How swift would be the coup? What does it mean for our future? What can realistically be done?

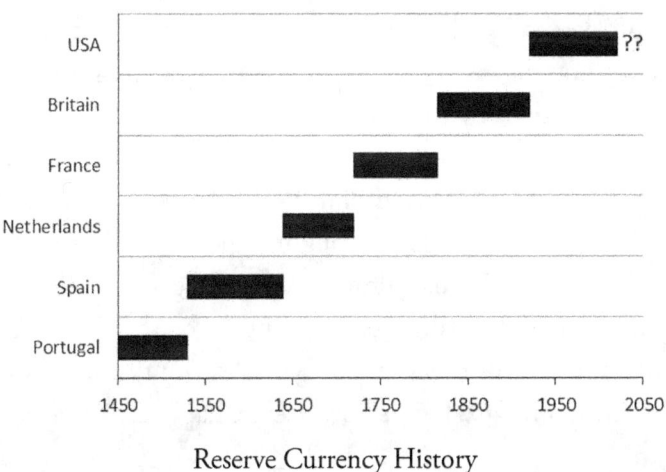

Reserve Currency History

Looking at historical end of life cases of currency debasement, we can conclude that collapse is always preceded by a long period of unattended decline, but when it comes, things happen very quickly. Take for example the case of the British pound sterling, the dollar's predecessor. Prior to World War I, the British Empire stretched throughout the entire world and a quarter of the world's population was under British rule. Britain's national debt was about 30 percent of its GDP, and one pound could be exchanged for four to five dollars. By the end of World War II, the debt-to-GDP ratio was 250 percent. With its coffers empty, within several years Britain was forced to relinquish most of its colonies, its military shrank to the level of a second tier power, and the world ceased to be at the mercy of London's capital market. With the United States becoming the emerging superpower, countries shifted more and more of their currency reserves from the Sterling to the dollar, leading to a 50 percent decline in the value of the British currency in the first decade of the post-war era. Today, one British Pound can barely buy 1.25 dollars.

A much earlier example of how quickly currency collapse can occur was the debasement of the currency of the Roman Empire, the silver denarius. During the first century BCE, the denarius contained at least 80 percent silver, but as the empire grew and with it the appetite for grandiose projects and frivolous spending, the purity of the denarius eroded. By the end of the second century CE, the silver content in the denarius dropped to 50 percent. But then, over just twenty years, between 244CE and 265CE, the silver content sank to less than one percent. This brought hyperinflation, soaring taxes and a collapse of the Roman-dominated trading system. Resentment among Roman soldiers due to the dilution of their salaries led to defections and the disintegration of what was until then the world's most powerful military. This is how decline happens: slowly and then quickly.

Are any of those historical examples relevant to 21st century America? Yes and no. For the past half century, the United States has been enjoying the benefits of an international rules-based system of its own creation, leaning on ideas like global alliances, free trade, laissez-faire capitalism, multinational institutions and treaties, freedom of navigation and the commitment to democracy and human rights. But recently things have been changing, partly due to Americans' own doing. Fed up with decades of futile and extremely costly wars and nation building, by one account roughly $6 trillion since 2001[3], many Americans believe the globalized system has failed to deliver the expected dividends, and they are asking their leaders to rethink America's grand bargain with the world. This trend is happening in both Democratic and Republican camps. President Donald Trump's push for more equitable burden sharing in the defense of Europe and Asia, his general aversion to foreign military adventurism and his strong preference for fair trade over free trade are part of the rethink. At the same time, there is no denying that, throughout the world, faith in the United States as guarantor of peace, security and human rights is fading. The Trump administration's America First agenda and its departures, and threats to depart, from multinational treaties, alliances and international organizations have shaken the world's confidence in America's commitment to lead. At the same time, the United States has become deeply anxious about the rise of so-called "revisionist powers" like Russia and China, both committed to challenging the U.S.-led system, but, as Evan Feigenbaum noted, "it's tough to critique another country's obvious revisionism when you're a revisionist yourself."[4] This change in America's approach to the world undoubtedly affects the world's faith in America and, as a consequence, its willingness to accept the dollar system. And yet, while chronologically the dollar is nearing the life expectancy of erstwhile reserve currencies, no other contender to the throne is yet visible on the horizon. If the United States remains the world's largest free economy and as long as Washington maintains the trust of numerous countries, the dollar's status could prevail for decades to come. The reason is that for all of its deficiencies the United States and its dollar system are still the most beautiful house in quite an ugly neighborhood. Consider the alternatives: the Euro? Too shaky; the Chinese Yuan? Insufficiently convertible and controlled by the non-transparent Communist Party; the Swiss Franc? Too small; the Japanese Yen? Overly leveraged; the Russian Ruble? Forget that.

But the replacement of the dollar by another single sovereign currency should not necessarily be viewed as the main danger. What we should rather concern ourselves with is the decline of the dollar's share in the global currency basket and in international trade in favor of a combination of other currencies—some fiat, some digital—backed by alternative platforms of exchange and data collection. This trend has been well underway for years. According to the

Department of Treasury's Borrowing Advisory Committee (TBAC), the dollar share of global foreign exchange reserves has steadily come down from 72 percent in 2000 to 62 percent now.[5] The IMF has concluded, too, that the international monetary system is transitioning from a bipolar system—in which two currency blocs dominate, i.e., the dollar and euro—to a tripolar one, which includes the yuan bloc.[6] If the erosion of the dollar's strategic status is already under way, the question is how long and how deep will it be? The shift toward currency multipolarity is consistent with the general change in the current world order as the balance of power underpinning it is becoming less and less acceptable to more and more state and non-state actors. As a result, the world is gradually turning into a multipolar system, with several powers vying for influence. It is now becoming increasingly clear that resurrecting the old order may no longer be possible. If anything, the challenge of the next several years will be managing the disintegration and preventing the global system from sliding into dangerous chaos. What we are witnessing today is a gradual redistribution of economic and geopolitical power with China and Russia, and to some degree India, itching for recognition of their respective spheres of influence while spearheading the formation of alternative global institutions which include among other things an alternative monetary system. A growing number of countries, multinational organizations, corporations and individuals have already argued that the dollar-based system has run its course, that the dollar has proven to be an unreliable store of value and that the U.S. government by virtue of the dollar's special status is using its economic power to coerce and intimidate the rest of the world. A new global reserve system should therefore be created, they argue, one that is no longer subservient to the dollar or the whims of Washington officials.

## Pushing back

The idea of reducing global dependency on the dollar as the reserve currency of the world is not a new one. In the 1960s, it was the Europeans who resented what they viewed as an "asymmetric financial system" where foreigners were called to support American living standards and subsidize American multinationals.[7] It was their vote of no confidence in the dollar, withdrawing their gold reserves from U.S.-based vaults, which led President Richard Nixon to extract the United States from the Gold Standard. In the 1970s, it was the Japanese yen that was viewed as the emerging challenger. Two decades ago, the introduction of the euro raised fears that dollar hegemony would soon be over. In between, enemies of the United States like Iraqi President Saddam Hussein, Libyan leader Muammar Gaddafi, Venezuelan President Hugo Chavez and Iran's Supreme Leader Ali Khamenei, each in his turn, called for ending the dollar hegemony, offering their oil for alternative currencies. Their actions never amounted to much and, with the exception of Khamenei, none of them survived long after.

But perhaps more than anything, it was the global financial crisis of 2007-09 that shook the world's confidence in America's economic resiliency. In 2010, as the world was recovering from the massive shock, the United Nations issued a report which looked at global development challenges. Signed by UN Secretary-General Ban Ki-moon, the report identified the dependence on the dollar as a major source of weakness in global economic governance. It argued that many developing countries accumulated vast amounts of dollar reserves during the 2000s, but to their detriment "the dollar has proven not to be a stable store of value, which is a requisite for a stable reserve currency." One of the drawbacks associated with the dollar being reserve currency, the report claimed, is that the global economy becomes tied to United States monetary policy, while the United States Federal Reserve manages monetary policy based only on the needs of the U.S. economy. The report implied that the United States was engaged in beggar thy neighbor policies that benefit itself at the expense of the rest of the world. Among its recommendations, the report called for the formation of a new global reserve system which would allow for better pooling of reserves at the regional and international levels. This system must not be based on a single currency or even multiple national currencies but, instead, should be based on more liquid and independent instruments.[8]

One year later, the International Monetary Fund (IMF), then under the leadership of Dominique Strauss-Kahn and also under the trauma of the global financial crisis, called for the creation of a new world currency that would challenge the dollar system and help curb financial instability. In a speech in Washington, Strauss-Kahn argued that the reserves that member countries held with the IMF, called Special Drawing Rights (SDRs), could be used instead of the dollar in international trade. "Using the SDR to price global trade and denominate financial assets would provide a buffer from exchange rate volatility," he said, while "Issuing SDR-denominated bonds could create a potentially new class of reserve assets".[9] This was music to the ears of many countries, some like Russia, due to their anti-American, revisionist tendencies, others like China and India, which saw an opportunity for their currencies to play a bigger role in financial markets and the IMF on par with the size and growth of their economies, while smaller developing countries saw the UN and IMF proposals as ways to diversify their reserve assets and get around various financial constraints imposed by the United States. Since then, the calls for de-dollarization have grown louder and louder and the idea is now espoused by a growing alliance of nations, multinational organizations and financial institutions while being cheered from the sidelines by non-state, nefarious actors like drug cartels, crime syndicates and terrorist networks. We will describe this alliance, its motives and some of its actions in the following chapters.

The pushback against the dollar is not only a result of the rise of others. Nor should it be viewed as some international conspiracy. We would do ourselves a great disservice if we ignored America's own role in undermining its own currency. As we describe in the next chapter, United States' control over the plumbing of the international financial system creates an irresistible temptation to use economic sanctions and other coercive tools as measures of first resort mainly in situations where diplomacy alone is insufficient but military force is not the right response. The United States has long been exercising what a growing club of countries perceive as overly aggressive economic coercion: imposing sanctions on a large part of humanity and extending the long arm of its law to impose its will, values and policies on the rest of the world. To put it bluntly, what we call the "rule of law" is viewed in some parts of the world as a new form of imperialism. As long as U.S. leadership was widely accepted, the world grudgingly put up with many U.S. dictates; the benefits exceeded the costs. But seeming indifference to international crises like Ukraine, Syria, Libya, the European refugee crisis, the Greek financial crisis, etc. furthered by strong rejection of globalization and the drift toward an unapologetic "America First" agenda have placed into question the legitimacy of America's hegemony in the eyes of many. It is worth paying attention to Russian President Vladimir Putin's observation on the American empire and the dollar. Granted, Putin is a deeply unpopular figure in America today, but his views reflect a growing sentiment abroad which can no longer be dismissed:

> An empire always thinks it can afford to make mistakes or incur additional costs. It thinks it is so powerful that this won't change anything. But those mistakes and costs keep piling up. At some point, the empire can't deal with them both in terms of security and the economy. That's what

our American friends are doing. They're undermining trust in the dollar as a universal payment instrument and the main reserve currency. So everybody started thinking of a plan B.[10]

As with many other slow moving threats, the push for de-dollarization is easy to dismiss, especially when the U.S. economy stands tall above all of its other competitors. We shouldn't. The growing repudiation of the dollar regime corresponds with another development: the out-of-control growth in U.S. federal debt, which has already reached $22 trillion and is growing at an astounding rate of roughly $1 trillion a year. (This does not include corporate debt, home mortgages, home equity loans, auto loans, student loans and credit cards together totaling roughly $30 trillion). Apparently, the dollar regime that has allowed the United States to run fiscal deficits and become the most powerful country on the planet is now under threat due to the very same deficits it enabled. Drawing from the experience of the fall of the Habsburg Spanish, Bourbon French and British Empire, historian Niall Ferguson observed that empires fracture and fall when the cost of servicing their debt surpasses their defense budget.[11] We are getting close to this point. Even in the current environment of relatively low interest rates, the United States spends $1.5 billion every single day on interest payments. This figure is growing at an alarming pace. A 2018 study by the Committee for a Responsible Federal Budget (CRFB) projects the amount of money the U.S. government will spend on servicing its debt will surpass Medicaid spending by 2021 and defense spending by 2024.[12] The Congressional Budget Office (CBO) estimates that in 2025 the United States will spend on debt payments more than it spends on all nondefense discretionary programs combined, from funding for scientific research, to health care and education, to infrastructure. By 2028, the interest spending will rise to $915 billion or 13 percent of all outlays and 3.1 percent of gross domestic product.[13] This terrifying figure does not include the amount the U.S. government has to spend on repaying the actual amount borrowed before interest costs are taken into account. It also does not take into account all types of exogenous events that may come our way and require a sudden and massive increase in spending: wars, natural disasters, pandemics and financial crises. Here again it is worth reflecting on the fate of the British Empire. Until World War I, payments for the annual interest on its debt stood at 2 percent of its GDP. By 1933, the year Adolf Hitler came to power in Nazi Germany, the cost of servicing the British debt was nearly 10 percent, denying Britain the necessary resources to prepare itself for the coming war. Now, as then, such a level of borrowing is unsustainable even if the United States lived up to all of its global commitments and was viewed by the rest of the world as a reliable debtor. But this is no longer the case. To be sure, international relations are based on national interests, but they also rely on trust. When a country trusts another country to repay its debt, it has no problem buying its bonds. But when the trust is shaken and the risk of default or war is perceived to be high, central bankers will expect higher yields or they will diversify their portfolio to bonds denominated in other currencies or to gold. If the world decides that U.S. debt is out of sync with its economic performance, and if faith in the U.S. leadership and political system continues to erode, more and more countries will consider deleveraging their dollar assets.

Much of what will happen depends on China, which currently owns almost a quarter of U.S. foreign debt. While today China still agrees, albeit grudgingly, to maintain its role as a major holder of America's foreign debt, one must be a hopeless optimist to assume that this arrangement can be sustained as the two powers are sliding into what seems to be a new Cold War. What will happen to the dollar when China uses its growing power to compel its trading partners to shift their bilateral trade with it to national currencies as it implements its plan to internationalize the yuan? What might be the impact on U.S. inflation, interest rates and our ability to finance our deficit spending? These are all questions we must begin to ponder. Unfortunately, the siloed nature of Washington, its short-termism and partisanship, make it difficult for our leaders to deal with slow moving threats that are both generational and multifaceted. Instead, our leaders prefer to rely on know-it-all economists and bureaucrats and indulge in a business-as-usual mentality, reassuring themselves that everything will be OK. "Treasury remains confident that overall demand for Treasury securities will continue to remain strong" is the mantra of the government regardless of many of the warning signs that will be described in the following chapters.[14] To paraphrase Nassim Nicholas Taleb, until Thanksgiving Day the turkey is confident feedings will continue as usual. U.S. administrations think—at best—in four-year plans; Chinese, Russians, Iranians, and others plan for much longer time horizons. Their various regimes may be younger than that of the U.S. but their nations are older and their leadership perhaps more wary of the lessons of history.

The plot to undermine the dollar will metastasize slowly over the tenures of several U.S. administrations and through most of this time the public will most likely be too consumed with daily noise to pay attention to the sound of termites feasting under the floorboards of the seemingly robust dollar house. An effective response would need to be clear, effective, durable and upheld by successive administrations. For now it is still possible to slow the drift. It may even be possible to arrest it altogether. The window of opportunity will not be open for long though.

# 1 WEAPONIZING CURRENCY

*The power of the U.S. today is not military,
it's the dollar. They squeeze you out.*
*Javier Solana, former NATO Secretary General*[1]

The United States has by far the most powerful military on the planet. This hugely expensive instrument of foreign policy is essential to ensuring global peace, prosperity and order. But in today's world the use of force is becoming increasingly unpopular. This is in part due to our growing aversion to casualties but even more so because modern wars are almost impossible to win. If in previous centuries wars were almost always decided on the battlefield, in the 21$^{st}$ century, when standing armies are called to fight against insurgents and guerilla groups, often using civilians as human shields, nobody ever seems to lose a war. But while democratic societies are becoming less tolerant of the consequences of military confrontation, there are always villains waiting on the sidelines to take advantage of our war fatigue, developing weapons of mass destruction, oppressing and massacring their people and supporting terrorist groups who wish us ill. The temptation to react is there, but our willingness to pay the price is not, unless of course direct

American interests are at stake. This is why in lieu of military conflict, economic punishments like sanctions and other trade measures have become the go-to solution in U.S. foreign policy.

Sanctions as an instrument of foreign policy are a double-edged sword. On the one hand, they are more popular, cheaper and easier to implement than the use of force. All that is needed is an act of Congress or presidential executive order or, when international consensus can be reached, a United Nations Security Council resolution. As President Woodrow Wilson explained a century ago: "It does not cost a life outside the nation boycotted, but it brings a pressure upon that nation which, in my judgment, no modern nation could resist."[2] On the other hand, as the economic penalties imposed on countries like Iraq, Iran, Sudan, Cuba, Russia and North Korea have demonstrated, sanctions have not proven to be terribly effective as a way of transforming a country's behavior. Sometimes they do, but in most cases not. At best they can be used successfully as a "diplomatic meat tenderizer" in preparation for tough negotiations, provided they are implemented smartly, in a multilateral fashion and in coordination with other instruments of statecraft.

U.S. economic statecraft has gone through an interesting evolution over the past two decades with regards to the use of sanctions. During the Cold War, U.S. sanctions targeted a country's entire trade with the rest of the world. So trading Cuban cigars, for example, would be a violation of the sanctions on Cuba. But since September 11, with the role of the dollar becoming more important, successive U.S. administrations turned from broad-based sanctions to more targeted financial sanctions. In other words, instead of intercepting the flow of goods around the world—cigars in the case of Cuba—the United States started intercepting the flow of money, punishing banks for facilitating payments through the U.S. dollar clearing system. A second innovation in the use of sanctions has been the shift from primary sanctions to secondary ones. Primary sanctions mean that no U.S. person can do business with a sanctioned entity. So, for example, bank X can be sanctioned for channeling money to a terrorist organization and no U.S. person or entity would be allowed to do business with that bank. Secondary sanctions expand the reach of the sanctions, applying them to non-U.S. entities. This way, a German company that wants to do unrelated business with bank X would face the risk of being cut off from the U.S. financial system. Thus, the U.S. essentially tells the world that it has a choice: abide by our unilateral policies or suffer what most corporations and businesspeople would consider a financial death sentence.

## Axis of resentment

U.S. law grants the president almost unlimited powers to sanction foreign states, entities or individuals. These powers go back to 1977 when Congress passed the International Emergency Economic Powers Act (IEEPA), authorizing the president to block transactions and freeze assets of those who constitute a "threat to the national security, foreign policy, or economy of the United States." This catch-all mandate is so broad that theoretically at some point or another numerous countries could find themselves on the receiving end of U.S. punitive measures just because their foreign policy is not to America's liking. Hence, the imposition of economic sanctions has become a kneejerk reaction to almost every transgression on earth. Harassment of an ethnic minority in Darfur? Sanctions. The International Criminal Court wants to prosecute Americans? Sanctions. North Korea testing a missile? Sanctions. Arrest of an American citizen in Turkey? You guessed it. The temptation to hit the world's villains in their pocketbook is strong. Sanctions are not only the president's option of first resort, they also provide Congress with an opportunity to reassert itself in foreign policy. Activist members of Congress often pick an international issue close to their heart—or the heart of a constituency—and champion it, urging their colleagues to support their pet legislation to sanction this or that. One becomes a champion of Tibet, another of the Copts in Egypt, and another of the Rohingya minority in Myanmar. With 535 senators and representatives, some 468 of whom are running for reelection every two years, and with a world that is becoming increasingly complex and fraught with dangers, bad guys worthy of being sanctioned keep piling up. No wonder the United States currently has in place no fewer than 28 sanctions programs. Think about it: one in ten countries in the world is under U.S. sanctions. These include Russia, Iran, Venezuela, Belarus, Burundi, Central African Republic, Cuba, Lebanon, Syria, Libya, Somalia, Yemen, Iraq, Sudan, South Sudan, Zimbabwe, Myanmar, the Democratic Republic of Congo, and of course North Korea. Other countries like Tajikistan, Angola and Honduras have either been under sanctions for various human rights violations or narrowly escaped them thanks to there being an important national interest for the United States. And then there are countries like China, Pakistan and Turkey that are not under any official sanctions program, at least for the moment, but for various reasons are the targets of other economic punitive measures like export controls, tariffs, embargos, etc.—which they view as economic weapons. Objectively speaking, almost every one of the sanctioned countries is targeted for what many Americans would view as a good reason, be it human rights violations, terrorism, crime, narcotics, nuclear proliferation and other unbecoming behaviors. China, which is not under sanctions—yet—but faces economic punishments Beijing views as indirect sanctions, has been notorious for cyber intrusions, theft of intellectual property and abuse of ethnic minorities and religious freedoms; Pakistan has harbored terrorists, including Osama bin Laden; and Turkey provoked Washington's ire for detaining an American citizen, for its treatment of America's Kurdish allies and for buying Russian weapons while being a NATO member. These are all actions Washington could not tolerate. The problem is that while each singular case is infuriating, if not outright injurious, and therefore merits some response, the aggregation of so many sanctioned countries, with a cumulative population of nearly 2 billion people and with a combined gross domestic product (GDP) of more than $15 trillion, has created an axis of resentment which, in turn, has triggered an unprecedented pushback against America's financial hegemony.

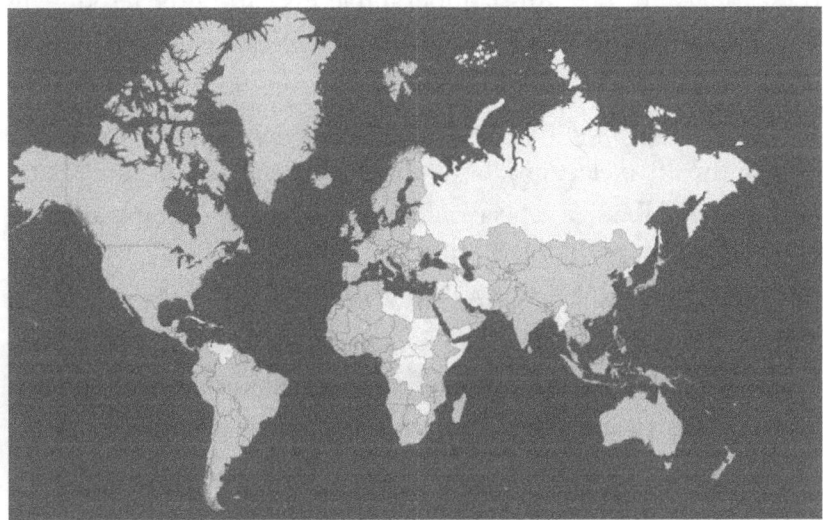

Countries under U.S. sanctions, 2019

U.S. sanctions also target tens of thousands of individuals, companies and state owned enterprises from scores of countries. The individuals and companies are often extremely influential and well-connected in their own countries; their ire with the U.S. has consequences. To understand how aggressive the U.S. has recently become in using sanctions, it is worth taking a look at the list of Specially Designated Nationals and Blocked Persons (SDN) under the Office of Foreign Assets Control (OFAC), a division of the U.S. Department of the Treasury. This list contains thousands of names of individuals and entities, and it is growing by leaps and bounds.[3] Since

2001, the number of entities added annually to the SDN list has grown threefold. In 2013, the list was 577 pages long. In 2019, the number of pages was 1,307. In the first year of the Trump administration alone, there has been a nearly 30 percent increase in the number of designations over the number added during President Obama's final year in office.[4] Many of those designated are either part of or are closely linked through family or business relations to their countries' leadership. Take Russia for example. As part of the response to Russia's occupation of Crimea, its involvement in the civil war in Syria on the side of Syrian President Assad rather than that of the U.S. and Saudi-supported Sunni insurgents, and its alleged interference in the 2016 elections, both the Obama and Trump administrations targeted Russian officials and businessmen who have strong ties to the Kremlin. A 2017 law called Countering America's Adversaries through Sanctions Act (CAATSA), which passed the Senate by an overwhelming majority of 98 to 2, required the U.S. Treasury to provide to Congress "identification of the most significant senior foreign political figures and oligarchs in the Russian Federation, as determined by their closeness to the Russian regime and their net worth" as well as an assessment of the relationship between those individuals and "President Vladimir Putin or other members of the Russian ruling elite".[5] In January 2018, the Treasury submitted a list of 210 prominent Russian political figures and business leaders including 96 "oligarchs" (the list was lifted from the *Forbes Magazine* list of world billionaires) none of whom have been charged with any crime. They just happen to know Putin and probably benefit from their relations with him. In April 2018, the Treasury unleashed sanctions against seven Russian oligarchs with ties to Putin along with 12 companies they own or control—again, to the best of our knowledge none of them charged with any crime—and 17 Russian government officials. This means that not only have their assets in the U.S. been blocked but also that U.S. citizens and residents as well as U.S. corporations are prohibited from engaging in any business with them. Administration officials admitted that the sanctions were not imposed in response to any particular event or crime but "in response to the totality of the Russian government's ongoing and increasingly brazen pattern of malign activity around the world."[6] But then a major escalation occurred. One of the sanctioned companies was Rosoboronexport, Russia's main arms export entity, which was placed on the CAATSA blacklist for its support of the Assad regime in Syria. In September 2018, under CAATSA authority, the U.S. imposed secondary sanctions against a Chinese military procurement company called the Equipment Development Department and its director for buying weapons from Rosoboronexport. In doing so, the U.S. extended its jurisdiction to the bilateral trade between Russia and China. These are not just any two countries. These are America's top two competitors and as we will see later, the two countries most committed to the de-dollarization effort. While in Washington the move got little attention, in Beijing it sparked a firestorm. It was one of the defining moments which brought China to realize that something must be done to protect its sovereignty.

**An American in Paris**

The long arm of U.S. jurisdiction is currently extended not only to governments and companies but also to the lives of countless individuals throughout the world. Thousands of people, for example, find themselves labeled by the U.S. Treasury as a "senior foreign political figure." Such designation, the American version of the international term PEP (politically exposed person), is typically applied to current or former senior officials in the executive, legislative, administrative, military or judicial branches of a foreign government. They can also be senior officials of a major foreign political party or senior executives of a foreign state owned corporation. In other words, any foreign person with substantial authority over policy, operations, money, or the use of government-owned resources in his or her own country could be labeled. But it doesn't stop there. Family members and close friends and associates of those "senior foreign political figures" may also fall under this category. Being on the list is no fun. For example, the niece or high school buddy of a senior official in, say, Mozambique would be exposed to intrusive and lengthy due diligence when opening a bank account or forming a company purely on the suspicion that the person has been directly or indirectly involved in pillaging his or her country's resources, laundering money or violating human rights. Could there be some bad apples among the thousands of "senior foreign political figures"? You bet. But is guilt-by-association a good enough reason to harm the lives and reputations of all the thousands of other designated persons, giving them reasons to shift their economic activity to the dark side of the moon, as far away as possible from the jurisdiction of the United States? It appears that the U.S. Congress and successive Administrations, convinced of the invulnerability of the dollar, have not bothered thinking through the cumulative effect of making it imperative for multitudes of highly influential people around the globe to find a way to conduct their financial lives entirely separately from a currency whose use subjects them to the jurisdiction of the U.S. criminal justice system and its threat to their wealth and freedom. The result is that each one of those people, their families and the companies associated with him, is reluctantly turned into another rebel in the insurgency that is building up against the dollar system. Nobody wants to be shanghaied at an international airport.

Slowly but surely, U.S. law is facilitating the growth of the insurgency. For example, the Global Magnitsky Human Rights Accountability Act of 2016 is adding new recruits. The act was initially signed by President Obama in 2012 to punish those responsible for the death in 2009 of a Russian tax accountant and whistle blower Sergei Magnitsky in a Moscow prison. The Trump administration made it applicable to any person around the world responsible for or complicit in, or who has directly or indirectly engaged in, serious human rights abuses. It authorizes the U.S. government to sanction human rights offenders, freezing their assets and denying them entry visas to the U.S. Since its implementation, more than one hundred individuals from fourteen countries have been sanctioned under the act.

Another constituency fed up with U.S. extraterritorial jurisdiction is that affected by the Foreign Account Tax Compliance Act (FATCA), a controversial law that was enacted in 2010, requiring all non-U.S. financial institutions to search their records for customers who are U.S. citizens or residents and to report the assets and identities of such persons to the U.S. government. Foreign banks that dared to refuse the U.S. government on the grounds of banking secrecy were notified that they would not be able to operate in the U.S., a poison pill to any respectable financial institution. It also requires U.S. persons to self-report their non-U.S. financial assets annually to the IRS. Other than Eritrea, the United States is the only country in the world which places citizens who live in foreign countries under its tax law. All other countries tax people based on the place of their residency—not their citizenship. FATCA aimed to fight money laundering, terrorism finance, tax evasion and other nefarious activities that occasionally occur under bank secrecy. It also promised to enrich the federal government by as much as $800 million in outstanding taxes. But like in everything in life, zealous enforcement brings unintended consequences. FATCA created a huge wave of resentment not only among the nine million U.S. citizens living abroad but also among banks and other financial institutions worldwide. The receivables came nowhere near the promised $800 million but instead imposed billions of dollars in compliance costs and accounting fees that were rolled over to innocent customers. So intrusive is FATCA that U.S. persons living abroad who have signing authority on foreign accounts or assets belonging to aging parents or disabled relatives or who are partners in foreign businesses must report on those accounts to the IRS even if their parents or business partners have nothing to do with the United States. The fines for non-compliance are draconian and so are the accounting costs imposed on those expats. Very few policies have caused as much international resentment of the United States as FATCA. It subjects holders of U.S. citizenship abroad to unfair treatment like double taxation, prohibitive compliance costs and other hardships including difficulties in opening bank accounts. Foreign banks have no choice but to conform to American demands. Failure to comply would effectively result in exclusion from the U.S., and by extension the international, financial system. This is a powerful stick. Fearing the high compliance costs and draconian fines imposed by the U.S. government for various FATCA violations, foreign banks are now viewing customers with ties to America as if they were citizens of Sudan or North Korea. Many prefer to simply not deal with Americans. It would not be an exaggeration to say that is easier for an Iranian passport holder to open a bank account or to issue a credit card in Switzerland than it is for a U.S. passport holder. Worse, to protect themselves from any possible mishap, foreign banks are closing the accounts of clients who have never thought of themselves as Americans but may have an American parent or some remote tie to the U.S. that makes them de jure U.S. citizens. A 2016 *BBC* segment featured Fabien, who was born in the United States and whose father brought him to Europe when he was a baby. He described his surreal situation: "I live in France; I work in France; my life is in France. I have no link to the United States. My life as a Frenchman is in France. I don't even speak English!" Yet, this accidental American cannot open a bank account or conduct normal business activity in his country of residence.[7] No wonder every year roughly 5,000 American citizens like Fabien choose to renounce their citizenship for fear of becoming casualties of the penal system of a country that is no longer their home—and will never be. The interesting thing about FATCA is that while the United States requires all other nations to share the fiscal information of their residents, it has refused to join the Common Reporting Standard (CRS) which was initiated at the G-20 summit in 2014 and which binds banks to share account information about assets with tax services of other countries. More than 110 countries have joined the CRS. The United States is the only G-20 member that has refused to join the standard. The result of this perverse situation is that foreigners holding their assets in the United States are much more protected than Americans holding their assets abroad. This may be lucrative for the United States' financial sector but the reputational damage to America due to this double standard is incalculable.

The long arm of U.S. law has for years targeted foreign companies operating in other countries under the Foreign Corrupt Practices Act (FCPA). The FCPA allows the Justice Department and the Securities and Exchange Commission to prosecute non-American entities and individuals operating abroad for bribes, kickbacks, money laundering and other unlawful practices. It aims to fight corruption and enhance transparency in order to level the playing field for U.S. companies competing against companies from countries in which the rule of law is lax. It also brings a lot of money to the U.S. Treasury. In the past decade, FCPA enforcement has intensified, enabling the government to collect from foreign and domestic companies and individuals found guilty of violating the FCPA roughly $1 billion a year in fines. But critics of the FCPA -- top among them used to be a Manhattan businessman named Donald Trump who called it a "horrible law" -- say it puts American companies at a competitive disadvantage and that its compliance costs are prohibitive. Additionally, most countries now have strict anti-bribery and corruption laws addressing bribery of their public officials, and even if their standards are not as high as those of the U.S., is it worth it for the U.S. to alienate so many international players by meddling in other countries' affairs? This price would perhaps be worth paying had corruption stood a chance of being uprooted from the world. But the opposite is true. Corruption is still extremely widespread. The World Bank estimates that over $1 trillion are paid in bribes each year and this costs the world more than 5 percent of its GDP. Under Transparency International criteria, there are more countries that are considered corrupt than those that aren't. And those who insist in remaining corrupt prefer to do business with likeminded regimes. For this they need to break free from the dollar. So while the United States fights against corruption, it also risks paying a heavy price in the future when it comes to the strength and acceptability of its currency. Our discussion here is not about right and wrong: it is about costs versus benefits.

## Controlling the plumbing

What gives the United States the legal right to extend its jurisdiction globally is the nature and architecture of the international financial system and the internet backbone supporting it. The way the system is designed today, most of the world's financial transactions transit in one way or another through the American economy. It is sufficient that a transaction anywhere in the world, even if between two entities which have nothing to do with the United States, is dollar denominated or processed through an American bank, including U.S. branches of foreign banks, to enable U.S. authorities to claim jurisdiction over the matter. After all, the dollar is the property of the U.S. government and any use of government property to perpetrate what the United States views as a crime makes it the business of its government. This enables the U.S. government to enforce measures like sanctions not only within its own borders and over its own citizens and residents but also over other countries and their citizens. If a German citizen bribes an African official using the American currency or wires him the money via a U.S. intermediary bank, this would be sufficient ground for U.S. authorities to prosecute him. Technically, U.S. jurisdiction could even be claimed for using internet servers located in U.S. territory to commit what America views as a crime. If emails are sent among a group of foreign conspirators located in Panama and those emails were somehow routed via American servers, U.S. authorities could claim extraterritorial jurisdiction and issue arrest warrants against the group. The fact that most internet traffic is routed through the United States, the fact that the dollar is the most widely used currency and that most international banks use U.S. based intermediary banks in wire transactions all give the United States power that no other country has today. It has not shied away from using it.

Why would all of these acronyms—IEEPA, FCPA, CAATSA, FATCA—be of any concern to America? After all, isn't the role of the United States to be a promoter of law and order, making the world more free, democratic and transparent? Yes, one can definitely make the case that as Winston Churchill said "the price of greatness is responsibility," that the "shining city upon a hill" must spread its light to the darkest corners of our planet. But we should also realize that American exceptionalism, commitment to fight all of the world's scourges and injustices and aggressive enforcement of U.S. law outside of America's borders come at a price. In our eagerness to punish the various offenders in our imperfect world, just because we can, we are creating a growing club of governments, corporations, politically exposed, wealthy and influential individuals, as well as millions of ordinary people who are fed up with what they view as an overly coercive financial and legal system. This club is growing at an alarming pace and it is nearing critical mass. Once new names are added to the club it takes a great deal of effort to remove them. Henry Kissinger explained the problem: "We publish a list of people who are sanctioned. So then, when the time comes to lift the sanctions, what are we going to say? 'The following four people are now free of sanctions, and the other four are not.' Why those four? I think one should always, when one starts something, think what one wants to achieve and how it should end. How does it end?"[8] Here is how it ends: today, roughly one of every four people on the planet lives in a country whose government is under some U.S. economic penalty. The vast majority of those foreigners have not been charged with any crime, not in their countries, not elsewhere. They resent America's extra-territorial overreach and they are getting really good at interacting with fellow sanctioned people, together figuring out ways to evade America's sanctions and hide their trades from U.S. regulatory agents who, in response, have to invest more and more resources responding to them. It's a whack-a-mole game the United States cannot win—and won't.

The biggest problem with America's aggressive use of economic penalties is the cumulative damage we bring on ourselves.[9] When the U.S. imposes unilateral sanctions, we expect the other countries of the world to follow our lead. If not, they too would suffer consequences through secondary sanctions. Their politicians and business executives could be facing limits on their freedom of movement, and in many cases their assets could be frozen. Their banks and corporations might be shunned from the American financial system and in many cases severely fined. In 2015, French bank BNP Paribas was forced into an $8.97 billion settlement for violating sanctions against Iran, Sudan and Cuba. In 2018, another French bank Societe Generale agreed to pay $1.34 billion to settle investigations into its handling dollar transactions in violation of U.S. sanctions against the same three countries. Other European banks like Credit Suisse and Standard Chartered faced a similar fate and so did Chinese telecom ZTE which in 2017 received a fine of $1.4 billion for its dealings with Iran. These fines went into the coffers of the U.S. government leaving millions of disgruntled Europeans and Chinese viewing America as a sort of toll-taking troll under a bridge. Increasingly, America's closest allies have become casualties of America's sanctions. When the Trump administration withdrew from the Iran nuclear deal and re-imposed the sanctions, European corporations were forced to divest from projects in Iran at significant cost to their shareholders. When in the summer of 2018 Washington imposed punitive tariffs on Turkey in response to Ankara's arrest of American pastor Andrew Brunson this triggered a market selloff not only in Turkey but also throughout Europe. And when in December 2018, U.S. authorities issued an arrest warrant against Meng Wanzhou, a top executive from China's telecommunication giant Huawei, for allegedly violating the sanctions against Iran and lying to banks, it was Canada that paid the price because the arrest and extradition procedure held on its territory exposed Canada to China's economic and political retribution, not the least of which were the detentions of Canadians Michael Spavor and Michael Kovrig. As an ancient African proverb says, when elephants fight, it is the grass that suffers.

What makes America's penchant for sanctions most problematic is the backlash - the emergence of an entire global industry of sanctions evasion and the development of a parallel financial system that can allow sanctioned entities to cooperate. The bigger the circle of sanctioned entities becomes, the greater becomes the motivation to violate them, dilute them or work around them. To use the words of Jacob Lew, President Obama's Secretary of the Treasury, who himself was quite active in slapping sanctions on numerous entities:

> We must be conscious of the risk that overuse of sanctions could undermine our leadership position within the global economy, and the effectiveness of the sanctions themselves. If they make the business environment too complicated or unpredictable, or if [we] excessively inter-

fere with the flow of funds worldwide, financial transactions may begin to move outside of the United States entirely, which could threaten the central role of the U.S. financial system globally, not to mention the effectiveness of our sanctions in the future.[10]

Indeed, unlike in the past, when each sanctioned entity had to face the consequences of its punishment by itself, today almost no sanctioned entity is alone. Governments, corporations and individuals under U.S. sanctions share a common goal and common tools to undercut them. And while building those tools takes time, some of them are already under construction. One example is the development of an alternative to SWIFT.

**Race to the SWIFT**

President Trump's decision to withdraw from the Iran nuclear deal, also known as the Joint Comprehensive Plan of Action (JCPOA), is one of the most controversial of his presidency. We will not debate here the pros and cons of the decision but what is beyond dispute is that it created a rift between Washington and most of its allies, not to mention Russia and China who were also signatories to the deal. What rattled them was perhaps less the breaking of the agreement without a clear proposed alternative as much as the economic punishments Washington promised to apply against those who refused to follow its dictate. Most controversial was Washington's demand that all oil purchases from Iran be terminated by November 5, 2018. The goal, as Secretary of State Mike Pompeo described it, was "to deprive the regime of the revenues that it uses to spread death and destruction around the world" and to compel it "to permanently abandon its well-documented outlaw activities and behave as a normal country." Failure to comply with America's new sanctions would expose the violating entity to secondary sanctions. Any financial institution, corporation or individual that would insist on doing business with Iran would risk being shut off from the American market. The decision unsettled Iran's top oil consumers: India, China, Japan, South Korea, Turkey and the EU. On the surface, almost all of them seemed to comply with the sanctions but below the surface some took measures to get around them. India and China shifted their oil purchases to rupees and yuans. European leaders, who as it is have deep antipathy toward Trump for many other reasons, announced the creation of a "special payment entity" to shield European oil purchasers from U.S. sanctions. But the main battle was fought over SWIFT.

SWIFT, the Society for Worldwide Interbank Financial Telecommunication, is a global provider of financial messaging services. It is based in a tiny city of La Hulpe in Belgium. Its executive staff and 25 board members are bankers, mostly European. Since its establishment in the 1970s, SWIFT created the standards that allow its registered banks, more than 11,000 of them worldwide, to transfer and exchange money and wire information under one unified platform. Contrary to common perception, SWIFT has nothing to do with the actual transfer of the funds. At no point in the international flow of money does SWIFT touch any money. SWIFT merely authenticates the identity of the sending and receiving banks, clearing the road for the transfer to take place. As a hub of information about international money transfers, SWIFT has become an important tool in the global fight against money laundering and terrorist financing. Its data is often used by U.S. authorities to gain information on sanctions violators. In 2012, when the EU and the United States still saw eye to eye on Iran, SWIFT disconnected Iranian banks from its system, essentially cutting them off from the global financial system. But in 2016 with the signing of the JCPOA, most of the banks were reconnected to the network. Trump's unilateral decision to mount a maximum pressure campaign against Iran brought

SWIFT back to the center of the debate. The Trump administration demanded that SWIFT disconnect Iran's banks again, but SWIFT, this time with the backing of the EU, China and Russia, declined. Washington then made it clear that SWIFT would be subject to U.S. sanctions should it decide to keep Iran connected. It also hinted it might ban SWIFT board members—all reputable international bankers—from working in the U.S. financial system if they helped Iranian banks defy U.S. sanctions. The threat worked. But a month after SWIFT disconnected Iran's banks from its system, it was back in the news. This time it was Russia that was in Washington's crosshairs. On December 6, 2018, a maritime clash between Russia and Ukraine in the Sea of Azov brought the U.S. Special Representative for Ukraine Negotiations Ambassador Kurt Volker to threaten to cut Russia off from SWIFT. It was not the first time such a threat was made. In fact, the head of Russia's second-largest bank VTB, Andrei Kostin, once said this would be tantamount to an "act of war."[11] The threat of being banned from SWIFT was also applied against China in 2017 by U.S. Treasury Secretary Steven Mnuchin who announced that Beijing's failure to follow the United Nations sanctions on North Korea would result in preventing its access to the U.S. and international dollar system.[12]

Washington's treatment of SWIFT as its own fiefdom has drawn the ire of many countries, leading to various efforts to introduce a competing system which is not subservient to U.S. arm twisting. Hence, in September 2018, Russia began to connect hundreds of its top companies, including its state owned companies Gazprom, Rosneft etc. to a homemade Russian equivalent of SWIFT called System for Transfer of Financial Messages (SPFS). Displeased with Washington's hardnosed approach, the EU also entertained creating a new SWIFT. German Foreign Minister Heiko Maas said: "It's essential that we strengthen European autonomy by establishing payment channels that are independent of the U.S., creating a European

Monetary Fund and building up an independent SWIFT system."[13] China too offers an alternative. Back in 2015, partly in response to reports originating from former NSA contractor Edward Snowden that the National Security Agency (NSA) was monitoring SWIFT traffic, the Chinese government introduced the Cross-border Interbank Payments System (CIPS) as an alternative protocol. CIPS is today a backup network for settling mainly trade-related deals in yuans although several Russian banks have already joined the platform.[14] CIPS and SPFS are nowhere near becoming as widely used as SWIFT. Even Russia and China themselves still prefer to use SWIFT over their own platforms. But today is today and tomorrow is tomorrow. The fact that there are already at least two mechanisms in place, in Shanghai and Moscow, to enable members of the de-dollarization movement to transact among themselves at will outside of U.S. jurisdiction teaches us an important lesson about sanctions: major powers cannot be treated like minor ones. When they are, they push back—and hard.

**Fighting lions with tasers**

Throughout the years, the United States has grown accustomed to sanctioning minor powers—Zimbabwe, Cuba, Sudan, etc.—which are heavily dependent on the global system. They have no say in the UN Security Council or in international organizations; their armies can be easily quashed; they depend on foreign loans and aid; and they could be easily isolated. Russia and China are a whole different story. Both share land borders with no fewer than fourteen countries; both have strong navies and armies, cyber and space capabilities, an industrial base and access to raw materials. Both have veto power on the Security Council and both are founding members of increasingly important international organizations like BRICS (Brazil, Russia, India, China, and South Africa) and the Shanghai Cooperation Organization (SCO) whose members they can mobilize at will. Chinese and Russian societies are resilient, nationalistic and easily manipulated by a central propaganda system. They cannot be brought to their knees easily. Years of sanctions on Russia did not prevent Putin from taking over Syria, solidifying his control over Crimea, tightening his bond with China, sowing tension in Europe and allegedly intervening in the elections of the world's number one democracy. He even managed to host—with great success—the 2018 World Cup. Not bad. China too should not be taken lightly. For all the international pressure applied on her on human rights, political freedoms, open markets, intellectual property and territorial disputes, China has proven remarkably unbending. China has a plan. It knows where it wants to be in 2025 and even in 2049, the 100th anniversary of its Communist Party. No degree of pressure, sanction, tariff, arrest or condemnation will divert it from its course. This is not to say that the United States should treat Russia and China with kid gloves. It shouldn't. But nor should we delude ourselves that lions can be fought with tasers. Sanctions should be used more judiciously and more carefully or else they will increasingly serve to prod the revisionists to initiate structural changes in the global financial system that over time will provide a viable alternative to more and more countries and entities within the sanction busting community. As Henry Kissinger said: "When we talk about a global economy and then use sanctions within the global economy, then the temptation will be that big countries thinking of their future will try to protect themselves against potential dangers, and as they do, they will create a mercantilist global economy."[15] And this, as the next chapters will detail, is exactly what China and Russia are doing.

# 2  THE DOLLAR BUSTERS

> The U.S. is the most powerful economy in the world. If we want to avoid dollar hegemony, the first thing we need to do is to avoid using dollars, because the foundation of the U.S. economy is based on the dollar reserves owned by other countries and this has given it the ability and confidence to press other countries to play by its rules. U.S. influence would eventually be weakened if we do so.
> *Russian economist and Putin adviser Sergey Glazyev, June 2019*[1]

In the next two chapters we will meet the main players in the de-dollarization movement. Some of these countries like Russia, China, Iran and Venezuela have already made a strategic choice to gradually de-dollarize their economies. Others like Pakistan, India, Turkey, Saudi Arabia and the European Union are sitting on the fence, weighing their options and watching with great interest the attempt to reshape the global monetary system. Those countries are increasingly concerned about the cracks forming in the old U.S.-led order, but mentally and institutionally they are not quite ready to jump ship, especially since there are no clear alternatives in sight. They will continue to conduct most of their trade in dollars but when dealing with fellow revisionist countries they will do so in alternative currencies. While most of their foreign exchange reserves will remain tied to the U.S. currency, they will gradually diversify their reserve portfolio away from the greenback and participate in alternative financial mechanisms. In other words, they will try to have it both ways.

**Russia**

No country has been more vocal and clear in its opposition to the dollar standard than Russia. Since 2014, when the United States and its allies used sanctions to punish Russia for invading part of Ukraine, Russia has been under various international sanctions. Throughout 2016 and 2017, Vladimir Putin still had hopes that a change in leadership in Washington, the economic decline of the Eurozone, Europe's need for cheap energy, and the European migrant crisis, in no small part originating from Syria where Putin is calling the shots, would ultimately create the impetus for sanctions relief. But neither the election of Donald Trump nor Europe's travails brought any change. In fact, things have been going downhill. The poisoning of a former Russian spy in Britain, Russia's turning a blind eye to Bashar Assad's ruthless crackdown on the Syrian opposition and further escalation in the Ukraine crisis only hardened the West's position toward the Kremlin. For Russia, the control over Crimea is a non-negotiable issue—Russia will never allow the Black Sea port of Sevastopol to become the home of a NATO naval base—and its dispute with Ukraine is therefore an irresolvable one. Despite Putin's desire to eliminate the sanctions, he knows that Russia might have to live with them for many years to come. "We're always getting new sanctions. They [the U.S.] deny us an opportunity to use the dollar," he complained.[2] Putin has had to develop a long-term strategy to deal with the growing rift with the West. He tightened relations with China, embedded Russia deeper in the Middle East and Central Asia and solidified Russia's leadership in multinational platforms from which the West is excluded like the Shanghai Cooperation

Organization, BRICS and the Eurasian Economic Union. Moscow has even tightened its relations with the Organization of Petroleum Exporting Countries (OPEC), historically a competitor, with the goal of achieving better coordination with the cartel on matters related to oil production and pricing. But more than anything, Putin became the banner carrier of the economic insurgency against the dollar. He declared his stated goal to "overcome the excessive dominance" of the dollar, and he put the entire Kremlin apparatus to work to achieve just that. "The reign of the dollar must end," said Andrei Kostin, the head of Russia's second-largest bank VTB. "This whip that the Americans use in the form of the dollar would then, to a great extent, not have such a serious impact on the global financial system."[3] Hence, in 2018, Russia became the first major country to announce a comprehensive multi-step de-dollarization program. The plan included selling almost all of its U.S. Treasury holdings—roughly $110 billion in total—and replacing the dollars with gold. Russia now owns more than $100 billion worth of the yellow metal.[4] It also included shifting import-export transactions from dollars to national currencies, mainly rubles, euros and yuans, providing incentives to businesses that resort to settlements in rubles, for example an expedited return of value added tax.[5] Surprisingly, Russia's call to its European trading partners to transition to settlements in euros did not fall on deaf ears. Such a transition was seen by the Europeans as a hedging strategy which could strengthen the position of the euro at a time the Eurozone's future is shakier than ever. Putin also impressed upon the Europeans that shifting their energy purchases from Russia away from the dollar would benefit European energy security because it would protect European energy buyers against decisions by the U.S. which might affect Russian banks and energy companies' ability to clear dollar settlements. Russia has also taken upon itself to broaden the de-dollarization alliance as part of multinational organizations in which it is active.

The architect of Putin's de-dollarization campaign is his economic adviser Dr. Sergei Glazyev. An author of forty books, Glazyev is one of the most influential figures in the Kremlin today. Born in Ukraine in 1961, he became a Minister of External Economic Relations under President Boris Yeltsin at the young age of 31. Twelve years later, he unsuccessfully sought the presidency of Russia as a champion of economic reforms, taking a hardline position against terrorism and corruption. After Putin took over the presidency, Glazyev announced his retirement from politics in 2007, pledging allegiance to the new czar. Once he was no longer viewed as a threat, his influence on the Russian leader began to mount. Today, Glazyev is one of the most hawkish of Putin's advisors, especially when it comes to the United States. He believes that the United States and Russia are on the verge of a global war and that the American capitalist system is breaking down. For Russia to prevail in this titanic battle, it must undermine the dollar system. "The more aggressive the Americans are, the sooner they will see the final collapse of the dollar and by getting rid of the dollar this would be the only way for victims of American aggression to stop this onslaught. As soon as we and China dump the dollar, it will be the end of the US' military might," he summed up his strategy in a 2017 interview.[6] Glazyev is not unfamiliar to the U.S. government. He was one of the first seven persons who were placed under executive sanctions by President Obama. As such he is banned from entering the United States. But this has only strengthened his position in Russia. In fact, Glazyev is one of the handful of potential successors to Putin, and should he one day ascend to power, de-dollarization will no doubt be an important part of his foreign policy.

Russia may have the world's largest landmass and the second most powerful military, but in terms of economic power it is not even one of the top ten countries. Many Americans who hear 24/7 about the "Russian threat" to their democracy view it as a seven foot giant with unending destructive power. In reality, Russia is more of an instigator than a great power. Armed with veto power in the UN Security Council, its power derives from its ability to disrupt, rather than build. Putin's entire strategy is based on the exploitation of weak, neglected and messy spots around the world, like Syria, Libya and Venezuela, establishing footholds there in the hope of turning them into future Russian vassals. To borrow from the investment world, he is a masterful dumpster diver in search of junk stocks. This strategy allows Russia to punch above its weight in international affairs and to become highly relevant in some of the word's nastiest hotspots. When it comes to the dollar, Russia should be viewed as a dangerous catalyst. In itself it cannot pose a meaningful threat to the dollar system. But by assuming a leadership role in the revisionist camp and through its sway over hydrocarbon and arms trading of about $1 trillion per year, Russia's efforts should be carefully watched.

**Iran**

When it comes to the backlash against the dollar, Iran is patient zero. The Islamic Republic has been under various sanctions since 1979, following the seizure of the U.S. embassy in Tehran. Since then, the country's international behavior has gone from bad to worse. It has become an epicenter of international terrorism, a proliferator of Shiite militant Islam and the developer of nuclear technology with which it has vowed to destroy Israel. With this, Iran became the only known case in modern history of a country's official policy being the elimination of a fellow country. No U.S. administration could remain indifferent to such behavior, and indeed successive administrations have spearheaded the global effort to confront Iran—militarily, diplomatically and economically. Ironically, the United States was also the one that gave Iran the biggest gift of all—the hope for Shiite resurrection. After fourteen centuries of Shiite oppression in the Muslim world, where Shiites are a mere 15 percent minority, it was President George W. Bush who offered the Shiites their moment under the sun by handing them the world's second largest Shiite center—Iraq - on a silver platter. The elimination of Saddam Hussein's Sunni Ba'athism effectively turned Iraq from a Sunni country to a Shiite one. This permanently tipped the regional balance of power in favor of Iran. It is important to remember that while the Shiites are the minority in the Muslim world, when it comes to the place that matters economically, the Persian Gulf, they are the absolute majority both demographically as well as in terms of economic power. This is because most of the world's oil reserves are located in territories inhabited by Shiites, not only Iran and Iraq but also the Shiite-dominated eastern province of Saudi Arabia, home to some of the world's biggest conventional oil fields. Since 85 percent of Saudi Arabia's export revenues originate from oil, trouble in the eastern province is the worst nightmare of the Sunni House of Saud and the oil market writ large.

For a brief moment during the last year of the Obama presidency, it seemed that Iran's pursuit of nuclear weapons had either been shelved, somewhat delayed or moved underground thanks to the JCPOA. The sanctions on Iran were lifted, and the country was beginning to restart its economic engines. But with the election of President Trump, Iran's luck changed again. Fulfilling his promise to pull the United States out of the nuclear deal, which he called "the worst deal ever," Trump put Iran back in the hot seat, instituting tough sanctions, which include secondary sanctions against banks that process payments related to Iranian oil transactions with the goal of reducing Iran's exports to zero. The impact on the Iranian economy has been devastating. Iran's currency has nosedived, sending inflation to 40 percent in 2018. But crippling as the blow may be, it is not at all clear that America's extreme pressure campaign would lead to an Iranian capitulation, especially if its leaders believe—as they do—that Washington's true agenda is regime change. Iran's other major trading partners have not only disassociated themselves from Trump's policies, some have also declared their intention to undermine the sanctions. This has boosted Tehran's confidence and motivation to hold tight and wait out the Trump administration.

The economic siege on Iran has made it a world champion in sanctions evasion. "If there is an art we have perfected in Iran and can teach to others for a price it is the art of evading sanctions," said its Foreign Minister Mohammad Javad Zarif.[7] Obviously, de-dollarization is at the core of Iran's survival strategy. The country's Supreme Leader Ayatollah Ali Khamenei said that the "dollar has no place in our transactions today."[8] Zarif elaborated: "America's power rests on the dollar; a great part of America's economic power will go away if countries eliminate the dollar from their economic systems."[9] Iran has been selling its energy resources for non-dollar currencies like euros, rupees and yuans. It enjoyed a 10 billion euro credit line opened by China as well as a special financial channel offered by Europe with a view to getting around the sanctions. In April, Tehran created the Special Trade and Finance Instrument (STFI), a financial mechanism for carrying out trade transactions without exposure to the dollar or to U.S. banks. It is also developing its gold sector, tapping into its estimated 340 tons of gold deposits in several large and medium mines. As described before, Iran's banks have been disconnected from SWIFT, so conventional financial transfers are difficult to make. Iran's strategy of survival will mainly rely on barter deals of sorts and smart management of the domestic front to ensure the economic pressure does not bring the population to a boiling point. In this, Iran's success will depend on the willingness of its top trading partners, China, India and Europe, to resist Washington's extreme pressure campaign which aims to deny the Islamic Republic the ability to export oil and metals.

## Europe

Despite the special and usually warm transatlantic relations, Europe has never really come to terms with the fact that the dollar is the world's reserve currency. Most hostile to the idea have been the French. French presidents from Charles de Gaulle to Emmanuel Macron repeatedly complained about America's running loose monetary policies at the expense of its European allies. It was de Gaulle's finance minister at the time and later president, Valéry Giscard d'Estaing, who referred to the dollar as "America's exorbitant privilege." President Nicolas Sarkozy made it a campaign issue to lessen the dollar's central role.[10] Emanuel Macron, felt more or less the same: "This is an issue of sovereignty for me. So that's why I want us to work very closely with our financial institutions, at the European levels and with all the partners, in order to build a capacity to be less dependent [on] the dollar."[11] Since it was the U.S. dollar that essentially rebuilt France after World War II, it sounds almost inconceivable that such a close ally has become champion of policies that aim to undercut the greenback. But this is exactly what is happening, and the sentiment is not only French. Germany, the Netherlands, and the UK are equally committed to European financial independence. In fact, it was because of Europe's run on the dollar in 1971 that President Richard Nixon decided to pull the United States from the Gold Standard, essentially giving rise to today's fiat money system.

It is no secret that on many issues, the U.S. and Europe's interests are no longer aligned. European leaders have become skeptical of America's commitment to Europe's security. Even EU Council President Donald Tusk, one of Washington's closest allies in the continent, said about the Donald on the other side of the Atlantic, "with friends like that, who needs enemies?"[12] What prodded Europe, America's number one trading partner, to make overtures toward the anti-dollar bloc was not Trump's withdrawal from the Paris Climate Accord, his attacks on NATO, his tariffs or his support for Brexit and other nationalist movements in the EU, but rather his May 2018 decision to withdraw from the Iran nuclear deal and reimpose the sanctions. To be sure, Europe is not thrilled by Iran's behavior. But it is not prepared to renege on its agreements and perhaps more importantly to give up on lucrative business in Iran. It is also fed up with Washington's unilateralism and its extension of extraterritorial jurisdiction, which causes massive headaches for Europe's banks and companies. Washington's unilateral sanctions on Iran and its threats to impose sanctions on European companies involved in the Nord Stream 2 gas pipeline, which aims to supply Germany with Russian gas directly via the Baltic Sea, has brought European leaders to draw a red line. Simply put, Europe is no longer willing to accept Washington's dictates or to subject its companies to the wrath of U.S. authorities. The sentiment is strong and conveyed frequently not by some fringe politicians but by most of Europe's mainstream leaders. Europe's snapback revolves mostly around the dollar. French Finance Minister Bruno Le Maire said: "I want Europe to be a sovereign continent not a vassal, and that means having totally independent financing instruments that do not today exist."[13] In September 2018, Federica Mogherini, the Italian politician who has served as High Representative of the European Union for Foreign Affairs and Security Policy, revealed plans to form a "special payments entity [...] to facilitate legitimate financial transactions with Iran and this will allow European companies to continue trade with Iran, in accordance with European Union law, and could be opened to other partners in the world."[14] Hence, in January 2019, Germany, France and the UK introduced the special channel called INSTEX—short for Instrument in Support of Trade Exchanges. The special system was conceived as a clearing house that could be used to help match Iranian oil, gas and metals exports against purchases of European goods in a barter arrangement. This way, no dollars would be used and EU banks would have no legal exposure.[15] Europe recognizes the risks of cooperating with Iranian financial institutions closely tied to the regime and subject to U.S. sanctions. It is therefore too early to tell how widely used the mechanism will be and what the United States will do to counter it. While Washington signaled that it would not shy away from hitting Europe for sanctions avoidance, it is unclear how vigorous its enforcement will be, especially since most major European companies have already chosen the American market over the Iranian market. In other words, Trump will have to decide how much he is willing to compromise transatlantic relations in order to crack down on Iran.

Nevertheless, the rift with Washington has already driven Europe to a new and potentially irreversible ideological mindset. Europe First, if you will. In December 2018, Brussels issued a blueprint to promote a stronger international role for the euro, one that reflects the EU's political, economic and financial weight in an increasingly multipolar world.[16] Among its many proposals, the blueprint called for intergovernmental energy agreements to be denominated in euro, a meaningful step considering that currently more than 80 percent of the EU's energy imports are priced and paid for in dollars. It also called for the development of a homegrown EU payment system. Regardless of the success of Europe's resistance, a Rubicon has already been crossed. Europe has never been truly loyal to the old financial order and moving forward it is likely to be even less so, though on the surface it will continue to pay homage to Washington. In this, Europe will become increasingly conflicted in its relations with China. As its economies continue to struggle, many European countries are likely to turn to China for salvation. This is already happening. In March 2019, as part of Chinese President Xi Jinping's visit to Rome, and to America's dismay, Italy became the first G-7 country to endorse China's major investment and infrastructure project, the Belt and Road Initiative (BRI). In addition to numerous commercial deals in an array of sectors signed during the visit, Italy was allowed to borrow money, in yuans, in China's $12 trillion bond market, effectively making China Italy's lender of last resort. Italy is not alone. Other countries may soon face a similar dilemma, and since money talks, they will gravitate toward Beijing and as they do so trading and borrowing in yuans will become an attractive proposition.

**Turkey**

For decades Turkey's dream was to join the EU and become part of the West. This dream is now dead. Despite being a NATO member, Turkey's relations with Brussels and Washington have become increasingly strained as Turkey moves further and further away from democracy and freedom. Under its authoritarian President Tayyip Erdogan, Turkey has become a serious regional challenge for the United States. This is mainly due to its attacks against America's Kurdish allies in Syria, its support for the Muslim Brotherhood and Hamas and its hostility toward Israel. Another flashpoint in the relations has been Trump's tariffs on aluminum and steel imports (those metals make up 10 percent of Turkey's exports) as well as America's reluctance to extradite Muhammed Fethullah Gülen, Erdogan's archenemy who is taking refuge in Pennsylvania. For a brief moment in August 2018, the relations nearly reached a boiling point over the detention of American Pastor Andrew Brunson, who was arrested on terrorism charges after the attempted coup against Erdogan in 2016. The faceoff with Washington led to a mini-meltdown of the Turkish economy. The Turkish lira lost a quarter of its value in one month, leading Trump to double the tariffs on Turkish aluminum and steel to 20 and 50 percent, respectively. Then, in January 2019, Trump warned Turkey of "economic ruin" if it attacked America's Kurdish allies in Syria after the U.S. had left the country. Such barbs should not be of much concern. What is more troubling is Erdogan's perception of Washington as a potential economic menace. His fear plays right into Putin's hands. During the faceoff with the United States, Putin was the first to back up Ankara, seizing the opportunity to recruit Erdogan to his anti-dollar coalition. It worked. Erdogan announced that Turkey was preparing to conduct trade through national currencies with China, Russia and Ukraine. With Russia settling in in Syria and making itself a permanent fixture in the Middle East, Turkey will strive to keep an independent posture and this means increasingly diversifying its economy away from the dollar, starting with limiting the use of the dollar in cross-border currency transactions. Turkey has already signed agreements with Russia and Iran for the exchange of their currencies, and Erdogan called for Turkish citizens to convert their dollar deposits to euros or liras in order to slow down the worsening exchange rate. He also urged the IMF to index its loans to gold instead of dollars.[17]

Turkey is increasingly interested in diversifying its economic and diplomatic relations away from the West toward the group that is challenging the established balance of power. This explains Ankara's decision to buy Russian S-400 anti-aircraft missiles knowing that such action would undermine its relations with NATO and exclude it from ever buying American F-35 stealth fighter jets. It also explains its interest in joining BRICS, an organization, which, as will be described in Chapter 5, has become the hub of the de-dollarization movement. As a member, Turkey will be able to intensify its relations with Russia and China, two powers with whom it shares a complex history. An alliance with two veto wielding permanent members of the UN Security Council can buy Turkey much needed diplomatic protection against mounting anti-Turkish Western sentiment. Additionally, more than 60 percent of Turkey's trade deficit is with BRICS countries. Turkey wants to enhance its economic integration with these five BRICS countries and increase its exports to them. It would be more than happy to do so in non-dollar terms. And while today Turkey is an embattled economy, its future may be much rosier. Turkey has a young labor force and the lowest debt to GDP ratio of all G-20 countries. In early 2019, Standard Chartered Bank projected Turkey to become the fifth largest economy in the world in purchasing power parity (PPP) terms by 2030.[18] As such, it could become a serious reinforcement to the de-dollarization bloc.

**Venezuela**

Venezuela was once one of Latin America's most affluent societies. It owns one of the world's largest oil reserves. It was even a founding member of OPEC. But for the past two decades it has become an economic basket case thanks to the reckless policies of its Marxist presidents, Hugo Chavez and his successor Nicolas Maduro. The country suffers from hyperinflation—80,000 percent in 2018!—and extreme food and medicine shortages that have sent millions fleeing to neighboring countries. Ever since the 2002 George W. Bush administration support for a coup against Chavez, Venezuela's relations with the United States have been intensely adversarial. In addition to economic sanctions by the United States against a number of people in Maduro's inner circle, including the first lady, defense minister, vice president and other allies, Washington has pondered forced removal from power of Maduro and it is reportedly preparing to add the country to the list of state sponsors of terrorism. In 2019, Washington ramped up its efforts to rid Venezuela of Maduro, announcing its support for opposition leader Juan Guaido as the country's legitimate leader and urging more than 50 of its allies to do the same. It also imposed secondary sanctions on financial entities facilitating transactions with the Maduro regime, and in the spring of 2019 the White House even hinted that a military intervention on behalf of Guaido was being seriously considered. Maduro has been defiant, and just like his predecessor, who expressed his intension to dump the dollar already in 2009, he picked the U.S. currency as his prime target.[19] In an attempt to skirt U.S. sanctions, Maduro shifted government auctions from dollars to alternative currencies like euro and yuan.[20] He also attempted to rescue the country's worthless currency, the bolivar, by introducing a cryptocurrency called the petro, supposedly backed by the country's vast oil reserves. It turned out to be a joke. The country's oil production has been in a free-fall and the specific oil field whose oil was supposed to back the petro is located in Atapirire, in the middle of the country and far from any infrastructure to ship the oil to market. It might as well be on the moon. In August of 2019, the United States imposed an embargo on Venezuela.

But despite the country's dire situation, it has remained afloat largely thanks to America's top two strategic competitors, Russia and China, who are eager to maintain a footprint in America's backyard. Russia secured holdings in large parts of Venezuela's oil and gas reserves as well as half of Citgo, Venezuela's refining company. Its national oil company Rosneft provided billions of dollars to Caracas as pre-payment for oil. In an effort to prevent the Maduro government from going bankrupt, Russia helped Venezuela launch the petro. China, for its part, provided a $5 billion loan and long-term oil purchase commitments.[21] It is easy to discount the fragile Venezuela. But should the Maduro government survive in power or be replaced by a more competent one, the country could snap out of its malaise in a relatively short period of time and use its oil sector to once again become a regional power. What its attitude will be toward the United States is difficult to predict. But should for whatever reason Caracas decide to return the favor to Russia and China, which supported it during the difficult years, it may end up becoming an important member of the anti-dollar axis.

## India

India is a pivotal country when it comes to the future of the dollar. The heavily populated country is projected by the middle of the century to surpass the U.S. economy in size to become the second biggest in the world after China. But until then it must struggle with severe developmental problems: poverty, energy insecurity and an environmental crisis. Air quality in India's biggest cities is so poor that it is estimated that more than a million deaths a year can be attributed to pollution.[22] Thirteen of the world's twenty most polluted cities are Indian. Despite its size, except for large coal reserves, India is energy poor. It is already the third largest oil consumer in the world and is expected to become the largest by the year 2040. As such, it will remain heavily dependent on the Persian Gulf for its energy needs. Iran is particularly important for India's future. Before the U.S. sanctions went into effect, it was India's third largest oil supplier, and as the world's second largest reserve of natural gas it could play a key role in India's effort to clean its air. If India needs Iran to win the war on pollution it needs China to win the war on poverty. Currently, India is apprehensive about China's rise and in particular about what it views as China's encroachment on its sphere of influence in the Indian Ocean and South Asia, especially in Sri Lanka, Maldives, Nepal and Bangladesh. It is also anxious about China's tight relations with its nuclear neighbor and adversary, Pakistan. At the same time, India realizes that good relations with China could make it a major beneficiary of China's infrastructure investments in South Asia, part of the BRI. One of the BRI's transportation corridors initiated by China, the Bangladesh-China-India-Myanmar Economic Corridor, is planned to connect the seven poorest Indian states, commonly known as the "Seven Sisters," to Myanmar and Bangladesh providing them with much needed access to the sea. For all its reservations about China's rise, India realizes the importance of staying on China's good side. The same is true for Russia on which India relies for remaining militarily independent and diversified.

Delhi's symbiotic relations with Iran, China and Russia weigh against its inclination to preserve its good relations with Washington.

India is likely to remain an important component of America's Free and Open Indo-Pacific Strategy (FOIP). It will also play a key role in the Quadrilateral Security Dialogue, also known as Quad, an informal counter-China security pact that includes Australia, Japan and the United States. But this is more or less as far as it goes. India has always prided itself on its independence and self-reliance. In the early 1960s during the Cold War, it co-founded the Non-Aligned Movement, a group of countries not officially aligned with any of the blocs, which insisted on maintaining their sovereignty and territorial integrity. As tension rises between the United States and China, Russia and Iran, India will—again—refuse to be dragged into great power rivalries, and like many other Asian countries it will seek to maintain good relations with all.

As a fence sitter, India is likely to be open to the idea of de-dollarization, at least partially. Its interest to a large degree is driven by its desire to internationalize its own currency, the Indian rupee, which currently plays a negligible role in the currency market but is likely to grow significantly as India becomes a major economic power. Today, however, much of India's attitude toward de-dollarization is driven by its approach toward Iran. During the last round of sanctions against Iran, India insisted on buying Iranian oil in euros as well as in rupees through a Rupee Payment Mechanism. It was essentially a barter system through which Iran could use rupees to buy Indian products, steel, medicine, food and chemicals. The U.S. pullout from the JCPOA and the reinstitution of oil sanctions put India again on the horns of the dilemma. To bypass U.S. economic pressure on Tehran, in November 2018, the Indian and Iranian governments signed an agreement for oil payment in rupees made through India's state-run UCO Bank, which has no U.S. exposure. The countries are also discussing additional barter-based mechanisms to avoid U.S. sanctions.[23] The relations with Russia are also de-dollarized. India recently bought a Russian S-400 advanced air-defense missile system and two warships and decided to settle the payment in rubles and rupees, not dollars.[24] The White House, which had previously threatened India with sanctions over Russian arms purchases, said the U.S. could give the deal a waiver from those sanctions if New Delhi only agreed to buy American F-16 jets.

In short, India will not lead the effort to transform the dollar system, but it is likely to be a willing partner for those who do. India is a key member of BRICS and as such it is de facto party to the group's de-dollarization program. When offered a credible and reliable alternative to the dollar, it will not turn it down.

## Pakistan

Since the September 11 attacks, Pakistan has been viewed by the United States as an important ally in the war on terrorism. In truth, it has been a disappointing one. While its mouth expressed commitment to regional stability and the war against jihadist groups operating in its midst, its arms provided aid and shelter to some of the world's worst terrorists. As we know today, Osama bin Laden himself was sheltered for years in eastern Pakistan under the watchful eyes of the Pakistani security forces. This duplicity was finally called out by President Trump who withheld economic aid from the country. As its relations with the United States have declined, Pakistan has grown closer to China with which it shares not only a common border but also what is often referred to as "all-weather friendship." Islamabad has received billions of dollars in Chinese loans to finance ambitious BRI projects including a strategic deep water port in Gwadar on the coast of the Arabian Sea not far from the entrance to the Persian Gulf and a north-south highway connecting China's western province of Xinjiang and Gwadar, essentially opening China's landlocked western provinces to the sea. Both projects are part of the China-Pakistan Economic Corridor (CPEC), a centerpiece of the BRI. In the wake of the deterioration of U.S.-Pakistan relations and Islamabad's drift closer to China, the two countries are gradually transitioning their bilateral trade, $15 billion annually, from dollars to yuans.[25] Looking forward, for the dollar revisionists Pakistan is a low hanging fruit to pick. It is already the sixth most populated country with a population growth rate on track to make it by 2030 the country with the single largest Muslim population. With 100 million people below the age of 30, Pakistan's economy is growing at a steady pace and its relations with China will continue to enable this growth, placing it on the list of the world's 20 largest economies.

All of the above de-dollarization efforts are interesting. But it is hard to see how a group of fence sitters and second and third-tier economies, even if working in concert, can transform the world's monetary system. There is only one country that is large enough, rich enough, ambitious enough and committed enough to challenge Pax Americana to shepherd the effort. It deserves an entire chapter.

# 3 IS RED THE NEW GREEN?

> Always be nice to bankers.
> *John Gotti*

China is the only country where traders cheer when the stock markets monitors are colored red. Red, the color of happiness and good luck in Chinese culture, means that a share's price has gone up, rather than down, unlike in other markets where green means that a share price has risen. This symbolizes the diametrically opposed nature of the Chinese economic system compared to America's. Much has been written about the gigantic proportions of the opaque and state run Chinese economy and China's ambitions to surpass the United States as the number one economy—in Purchasing Power Parity (PPP) terms China has already done so—as well as to dominate the 21$^{st}$ century knowledge economy. If there is a single country that could truly challenge the dollar system, it is China. Such a suggestion sounded almost fantastic until recently, but the recent deterioration in U.S.-China relations has made it a real possibility. No doubt the Communist Party of China (CPC) headed by Xi Jinping since 2012 has done an admirable job enabling hundreds of millions of Chinese to lift themselves from poverty to the middle class, but prosperity has failed to bring China into the fold of democratic nations as many Western policymakers had anticipated. In fact, the exact opposite has happened. China has become more authoritarian, and the CPC's grip over the economy has tightened. China is becoming increasingly assertive and ready to challenge the United States economically, diplomatically and militarily. So after four decades of hope that as China developed with the help and encouragement of the United States it would open its economy and embrace political reforms, Washington has reached the conclusion that the friendly and seemingly harmless kitten called China is turning into a potentially dangerous tiger that needs to be declawed before it reaches full size. This is why after eight presidents who treated China as a partner, the Trump administration officially rebranded it as "strategic competitor," and since early 2018 the United States has been engaged in what could be described as a full-blown all-of-government China containment strategy which spans all elements of national power: military, economy, technology, law enforcement, etc.[1]

U.S.-China relations are burdened with a slew of tensions including the maritime disputes over the South China Sea and the East China Sea, the independence of Taiwan, the future of Hong Kong and China's treatment of ethnic minorities in Tibet and Xinjiang Province. But more than any of these, it is the bilateral economic and trade relations that rattle the world. The Trump administration has some valid reasons for its desire to change the status quo and force Beijing into new type of relationship based on fairness and reciprocity. Following the lead of corporate America, which tried to tap into the world's largest consumer market, previous administrations preferred to turn a blind eye to theft by some Chinese of intellectual property and to cyber attacks as well as the Chinese government's numerous barriers to market penetration by American companies. Trump, by contrast, was ready from day one in office to "break some China" and challenge Beijing, and unlike on any other issue, when it comes to confronting China he enjoys strong bipartisan support in the U.S. Congress.

At the base of Washington's grudge against China lies the following argument: China manages its economy via tightly controlled state owned enterprises (SOE) and the state banks supporting them. This poses an insurmountable challenge to America's competitiveness. The construction, defense, heavy manufacturing, mining, shipping and energy conglomerates are all supported by the Chinese government in ways no Western company could even dream of. When Chinese SOEs bid for projects in Africa, they bring with them not only their technical and logistical skills but also the deep pockets and credit lines of China's banks, insurance companies, as well as cheap labor and foreign aid. In some cases, they even offer diplomatic concessions, bribes and other questionable goodies. Under such conditions very few American companies can compete and even fewer can win. American companies operating in China itself face similar unfair competition, and their only chance for success is by teaming up with strong local partners who often take advantage of the foreigners, exacting prohibitive cost in terms of equity and control of intellectual property. So when Washington talks about "structural changes," it is essentially demanding that China abandon important elements of its statist approach toward its economy and move closer to the American way of doing business. Another grievance by the U.S. is the trade imbalance between the two countries. Simply put, for all its size, China imports from the U.S. much less than the U.S. imports from China, leading to a giant trade deficit of over $350 billion a year. The U.S. wants China to reduce much of this trade deficit by importing more American products. Here, actually, the very same statist approach Washington resents so much can suddenly can become handy. The SOEs can simply be ordered by Beijing to buy more American soybeans or oil, and Chinese state banks can be told to finance those acquisitions. This begs the question: which China do we prefer? One governed by free market forces or one where the government dictates to companies what to buy and from whom?

In China's mind, Washington's demands are unacceptable as they are no less than a call to arms against the very existence of the CPC and against what China perceives as its legitimate and peaceful rise. China desperately needs domestic stability in order to complete its ascendance. Nothing worries its leaders more than social discontent which could be caused by an anemic economy. On the other hand, Beijing is extremely averse to rapid and forced-from-the-outside structural reforms. China's leadership culture adheres to Deng Xiaoping's dictum "cross the river by feeling the stones," meaning that forward movement should always be slow, grounded and incremental. Considering the country's size, complexity and tragic experience with reforms (think Great Leap Forward and the Cultural Revolution), sudden changes amidst uncertainty are always viewed as precarious and undesirable. All of this to say that the strategic arm wrestling between Washington and Beijing is not likely to end in the surrender of either side and is likely to transcend any single trade deal, comprehensive though it may be. The more likely outcome of Washington's ideological snapback is a protracted Cold War-style clash of titans, mostly on the economic front, with no clear winner in the end—only losers.

What few Americans realize is that much of what is happening today between the United States and China has its roots in the global financial crisis of 2008. Then, China was in the midst of a historic economic growth spurt, making final preparations for its official foray onto the global stage—the Beijing Summer Olympics. China was not as integrated in the world's financial system as it is today, and it had little understanding of the implications for its own future of Wall Street's risky financial acrobatics. When the crisis came, the shock was as intense in Beijing as it was in New York. It was the first time that the Chinese were exposed to the dark side of America's economic system, that is, the incentives to bad behavior caused by systemic socialization of risks coupled with privatization of rewards as well as the revolving door regulator/regulatee relationship leading to a regulator incentive system not so different from that articulated by former Saudi Ambassador to the U.S. Prince Bandar bin Sultan, who once observed of U.S.-Saudi relations: "If the reputation [...] builds that [we] take care of friends when they leave office, you'd be surprised how much better friends you have who are just coming into office."[2]

In fact it was a turning point in how China viewed the United States. Suddenly, the emperor had no clothes. Within several months of the collapse of Lehman Brothers, China's exports plummeted almost 30 percent and 20 million workers lost their jobs, triggering an exodus of biblical proportion from China's urban manufacturing hubs back to the rural areas. The near collapse of Wall Street came on top of another catastrophe a few months earlier in China when a powerful earthquake hit Sichuan Province, killing tens of thousands and causing damage estimated at $150 billion. The broad-based effect on the country from the shocks in Wall Street and Sichuan was profound. It was punctuated by a series of bestsellers, *Currency Wars 1, 2 and 3*, published in China by author Song Hongbing, who argued that the U.S. financial system is controlled by a clique of bankers who use the dollar hegemony as a way to lend money to developing nations only to subsequently short their currencies for quick gain, causing incalculable damage to the effected societies. It also claimed that the Fed is not really an independent body but the handmaid of those private banks. While in the West Song's claims sounded conspiratorial they had a deep impact on the minds of many Chinese thinkers and policymakers.

The CPC's response to the global financial crisis was fast and decisive. First, it sent the United States a lifeline, gobbling more than half of the $600 billion worth of Treasuries the United States offered to the world's central banks - important assistance that can no longer be counted upon under the current relationship should the United States find itself again in trouble. Second, it implemented a massive stimulus in its own economy, putting its SOEs to work on large-scale infrastructure projects like ports, high speed rail, roads and bridges as well as massive urban development programs, not to mention fixing the damage in Sichuan. For some perspective of the magnitude of the stimulus: during the years 2011-2013 alone, China used more concrete than the United States used during the entire 20$^{th}$ century.[3] The government's growth-centric policies, its industrial agenda backed by fiscal, financial and trade tools worked like charm. While the United States was undergoing the slowest recovery in history, China's GDP growth quickly bounced back. But a few years later, when China's growth began to taper, it was left with massive industrial output capacity surpluses in traditional industries like steel, cement, housing, shipping, etc. By 2013, Beijing began to realize that the same excess capacities that were originally created in response to America's financial crisis—ironically those surpluses now at the center of U.S. grievances—could spell trouble for its own future development. Laying off the millions who had just risen from poverty and sending them back to their villages was not an option. The gigantic SOEs had to be kept busy or else the ruling party could face trouble. Thus was born the Belt and Road Initiative.

## One belt, one road, several currencies

In 2013, President Xi Jinping announced an ambitious trillion dollar plan aimed at connecting Asia, Europe and Africa in a vast network of trans-boundary infrastructures—bridges, roads, pipelines, ports, fiber-optic lines and high-voltage power lines. The rationale for the plan was simple: building infrastructure in developing Asia, Africa and parts of stagnating Europe would stimulate those economies and this, in turn, would facilitate more trade with China. It would also offer China's less developed western, northern and southwestern provinces—Sichuan being one of them—easier access to new markets. The SOEs would be able to export their capacities to 70 countries in the vast BRI territory and China's banks would finance all that. This way everybody wins: developing countries enjoy better infrastructure and connections to new markets, the SOEs remain busy and content and China enjoys the prosperity that comes with enhanced connectivity and new markets. In short, the tide lifts all the boats. The Belt and Road, which included both land and maritime routes, quickly became the hallmark of China's domestic and foreign policy. It became so central that in 2017 it was enshrined in the Chinese constitution. If implemented as advertised—this is a big if—the BRI will be the biggest economic development program in history—more than ten times bigger in money terms than the Marshall Plan for the reconstruction of Europe after World War II.

America's response to the BRI has evolved over the past five years from cautious acceptance to outright rejection. During the Obama years Washington treated the initiative with ambivalence. It refrained from endorsing it but did not oppose it publicly. Behind the scenes things were less cordial. The Obama administration lobbied its allies not to join the Asian Infrastructure Investment Bank (AIIB) formed by China to finance and support BRI projects. It failed. One by one, America's allies joined the bank, and by 2019 nearly one hundred countries were members. This opposition to the AIIB was referred to by former U.S. Treasury Secretary Lawrence Summers as "the moment the U.S. lost its role as the underwriter of the global economic system."[4] The Trump administration was more curious about the BRI. Initially. In May 2017, a White House delegation attended the inaugural Belt and Road Forum for International Cooperation in Beijing, China's top international gathering for that year, expressing support for American firms' participation in BRI projects.[5] "The United States recognizes the importance of improving economic connectivity through high-quality infrastructure development, and hence, welcomes efforts from all countries, including China, in achieving this," said Matthew Pottinger, the National

Security Council director for Asia-Pacific who led the delegation.[6] But one year later, the U.S. position on the BRI took a 180-degree turn. The BRI suddenly became a symbol of Chinese expansionism and coercion, and China was blamed for using state capital to lure developing countries into dependency relations, applying predatory loan practices to mire nations in so-called "debt traps," and by this denying them long-term growth. Vice President Mike Pence maligned the initiative, referring to it as a "dangerous […] one-way road," signaling Washington's intention to counter it as it has since.[7]

## The mother of all debt traps

China has another perspective on the meaning of "debt trap." For Beijing, the mother of all debt traps is the United States of America, and it is critically important to understand this point of view in order to understand the interplay among the new Cold War, the BRI and the future of the dollar. For years, much of China's enormous trade surpluses with the United States—yes, the very same ones the Trump administration wants to eliminate—were ploughed back into the U.S. economy though the acquisition of U.S. Treasuries. In 2008, as part of its response to the financial crisis, China surpassed Japan as America's number one debt owner. Today the People's Bank of China owns roughly $1.1 trillion in U.S. Treasuries and another $300 to $400 billion in debt of government sponsored enterprises like Fannie Mae and Freddie Mac. Add to this, U.S. debt held by China via subsidiaries in places like Hong Kong and Belgium and the total amount is well over $1.5 trillion—roughly one quarter of total U.S. foreign debt. Roughly half of China's $3 trillion foreign exchange reserves are invested in U.S. Treasuries, down from nearly 80 percent in 1995.[8] But while Washington has identified Beijing as public enemy number one, as U.S. debt grows, China is expected to buy more and more of it. Washington is so confident in China's insatiable appetite for its debt that when asked whether he is worried about the possibility of

China pulling back on U.S. bond purchases in response to the administration's tariffs, Trump's Treasury Secretary Steven Mnuchin said he's "not concerned at all."[9] He should be. Very.

Today China is undergoing an intense internal debate about what to do with America's debt. Beijing is not likely to dump its Treasuries as Russia has recently done. This would be self-defeating. After all, its economy is still closely intertwined with America's, and with roughly $800 billion a year of bilateral trade on the line it cannot afford to make sudden moves. "This is very dangerous, like playing with fire," said China's ambassador in Washington Cui Tiankai when asked about the possibility as trade tensions worsened.[10] And even if it were in China's interest to do so, it would not be possible for Beijing to find a buyer for such a huge amount of U.S. Treasuries unless it offered them at a heavy discount. But the debate is not about dumping the treasuries China already owns. It is about the wisdom of rolling over those that mature. Currently China has not a scintilla of appetite for increasing its current holdings to the levels needed to meet the steadily growing U.S. fiscal needs. In fact, since the beginning of the trade war, its holding of U.S. bonds has been steadily declining.

China's holding of U.S. Treasury bonds has peaked

To understand China's dilemma there is no escape from delving into some numbers. U.S. federal debt currently amounts to over $22 trillion. Under the baseline scenario of the Congressional Budget Office (CBO), the U.S. federal deficit is projected to grow between 2018 and 2028 at an average rate of $1.2 trillion a year, adding a total of $12 trillion to the national debt. This means the total debt held by the public in 2028 will reach $33 trillion. Let's repeat this number - $33 trillion. Over the past 50 years, the annual deficit has averaged 2.9 percent of GDP, but going forward, from 2023 through 2028, it is projected to fluctuate between 4.6 percent and 5.2 percent. One does not need to be a member of the Tea Party to understand that these numbers pose a clear and present danger to America's future. What millions of Americans have not internalized yet is very clear to the technocrats in Beijing: soon the United States will no longer be able to borrow so easily the amount of money it needs to finance its budgetary obligations. The interest payments would simply become prohibitive. The cost of servicing $33 trillion of debt would necessarily chip away at growth and domestic investments. Here are some numbers to ponder: Of the $15 trillion in federal debt held by the public in 2018 (as opposed to the other $6 trillion held by various government agencies, including the Medicare Trust Fund, the Social Security Trust Fund, etc.), 57 percent ($8.5 trillion) was held by domestic investors and 43 percent ($6.5 trillion) was held by foreign investors. China as of this writing owns 23 percent of that $6.5 trillion. Japan holds more or less a similar portion. At the current growth rate of debt, the federal government will have to borrow on average $1.2-1.4 trillion each year.[11] This means that if China is to maintain more or less the same proportion of U.S. debt holding, it will be expected to increase its holding from $1.5 trillion to over $2.2 trillion by 2028. This means increasing its holding of U.S. Treasuries by an *additional* $70 billion every year.

How long do we think China will agree to fund the very same U.S. military that is preparing to fight it, the education system that is striving to outsmart it and that is closing its gates to Chinese students, the research and development infrastructure that aims to undercut its technology development programs and the Department of Justice lawyers who are prosecuting its companies? To paraphrase Lenin, China is no longer willing to pay the capitalists for the rope on which they plan to hang it. Even if the relations were great, China would still be unable to finance America's spending feast. In what the *Wall Street Journal* called a "tectonic shift" in China's economy, China's trade surplus with the rest of the world is shriveling.[12] This implies that what once was a nation of savers, with the highest saving ratio in the world, is turning into a nation of spenders. While still an export powerhouse, China is generating more and more of its growth from domestic spending. In other words, China is turning into America. For the United States, the implication of China becoming a consumption-driven economy is that it would have less of a dollar surplus with which to buy U.S. Treasuries.

Naturally, if China decelerates its debt buying, the U.S. will be forced to seek alternative buyers. The problem is that with the erosion in trust in the U.S. and its currency on the one hand, and the slowing down in global growth on the other, there may not be many takers. Japan's slow growth and aging population means that it too may not be able to keep up with the growing budgetary needs of the U.S. government. The third largest foreign holder of U.S. debt, with more than 10 percent of the total, roughly $700 billion, is not a country but FAANG, which stands for Facebook, Apple, Amazon, Netflix and Google—five top American corporations that keep their profits abroad in low tax havens like Ireland, Luxembourg and the Cayman Islands. These billions are being gradually repatriated to the United States, taking advantage of Trump's 2017 Tax Cuts and Jobs Act, which lowered their corporate tax burden. Since FAANG's money is heading home, rather than being funneled into purchases of more U.S. Treasuries, the salvation will not come from there. The rest of America's foreign debt is lodged in the UK, Brazil, Singapore, Saudi Arabia, South Korea, Switzerland, India, Canada, France and elsewhere, but most of them are either reducing their Treasury holdings or have no capacity to increase them by much. For the bureaucrats at the People's Bank of China, the gap between America's fiscal needs and the willingness and the ability of the rest of the world to meet them is glaring. What is baffling to them is the American media and politicians' indifference to the coming train wreck. Could it be that these smart Americans can't read numbers?

**Table 1: Top ten foreign holders of US treasuries, May 2019**

| Country | Amount of debt (in billion $) |
| --- | --- |
| China (including Hong Kong and reserves held in Belgium) | 1,347 |
| Japan | 1,101 |
| Ireland, Cayman Island and Luxemburg (mostly FAANG) | 715 |
| United Kingdom | 323 |
| Brazil | 305 |
| Saudi Arabia + other GCC | 273 |
| Switzerland | 231 |
| Taiwan | 172 |
| India | 156 |
| Singapore | 150 |

Like it or not, China is the only foreign country that has the capacity to finance America's spending, a fact that most policymakers choose to ignore. And the concern is—again—not that China dumps its existing U.S. Treasuries but that it declines to buy *more* of them. Without China's willingness to gobble more debt all that is left is the lender of last resort—the Fed and the U.S. government itself—and that too would have consequences, described later in this book. If China decides not to underwrite more U.S. debt, the U.S. will be forced to raise the yields on its bonds, but this means higher cost of debt servicing which means less money for defense, education, health, etc. Remember Niall Ferguson's theory that empires fracture and fall when the interest on debt surpasses the defense budget?

From China's standpoint, this is already a foregone conclusion. Pouring more money into the American debt hole makes no sense. It prefers to diversify away from dollar reserves into other assets like gold (since the trade war began, China has been gobbling gold like never before[13]), while redirecting more and more of its money to other foreign investments. The BRI is therefore China's mechanism for reallocating its large foreign exchange assets away from what it views as the American debt trap into more profitable and growth yielding infrastructures and technology investments. China has already made its decision: its money is going to build China and its Asian neighbors—not finance reckless spending in America.

## Three strikes

Zhou Xiaochuan is one of China's economic luminaries. For the fifteen years prior to his retirement in March 2018, he was the governor of the People's Bank of China. In this capacity he oversaw China's economic miracle and charted its monetary policy. Zhou is also known as a reformist who has been advocating for the extraction of China from the dollar dependency. On March 24, 2009, still under the influence of the global financial crisis, Zhou got the attention of the world financial community when he gave a speech titled "Reform the International Monetary System" in which he warned about the undesired consequences of overconcentration of foreign assets denominated in dollars. He called for the creation of a reserve currency that is disconnected not only from the dollar but from any individual nation and one that can remain stable over the long run.[14] This sentiment has been echoed by many Chinese scholars and policymakers over the past ten years since Zhou's historic speech, albeit with no particular sense of urgency.

Things changed toward the end of 2017 as it suddenly dawned on Beijing that the United States and China may be heading toward confrontation. In the midst of a nerve-wracking trade spat, several events crystalized China's understanding that something needs to be done to break free from the dollar system. First, was the arrest and trial of Patrick Ho, former Hong Kong politician turned businessman and scholar who was convicted by a New York jury for violating the FCPA by bribing top African officials in Chad and Uganda on behalf of a Chinese oil company. What gave U.S. authorities the jurisdiction to interfere in a business deal that was purely between African and Chinese nationals was the fact that the bribery payments were made in dollars—property of the U.S. government—and payments were wired via a U.S. intermediary bank. The second incident was the near-death experience of a large Chinese telecommunication company called ZTE. The U.S. government banned American companies from selling parts and software to ZTE for seven years in response to violations of a previous agreement under which the Chinese company paid $890 million in fines and penalties after it pleaded guilty to conspiring to violate U.S. sanctions by illegally shipping goods containing U.S.-made components to Iran. The ban was catastrophic since U.S. firms are estimated to provide 25-30 percent of the components used in ZTE's equipment. The crisis was finally settled thanks to Xi's direct appeal to Trump to save the 75,000 Chinese jobs the company provides. But then, in December 2018, came the third and most painful strike against China with the arrest in Canada—upon a U.S. extradition request—of Meng Wanzhou, the chief financial officer of Huawei Technologies, China's equivalent of Apple. Meng was accused of concealing from banks the true relations between a Huawei subsidiary which allegedly did business with Iran and the mother company. What made the story particularly explosive in China was the fact that Meng is the daughter of Huawei's legendary founder Ren Zhengfei. In May 2019, the Trump administration decided to ratchet up the pressure on China, issuing a ban on the sale of components to Huawei by U.S. suppliers. Even Google announced that it would be complying with the U.S. government's edict by suspending its Android services to Huawei's international customers. America's attacks on Huawei, which for many Chinese is a symbol of their country's progress and excellence, ignited deep hostility and nationalist fervor. The sale of Huawei phones soared while those of Apple shrank. The Chinese translation of a French book titled *Le Piege Americain* (*The American Trap*) detailing the ordeal of former Alstom executive Frederic Pierucci who was imprisoned in the U.S. for FCPA violations on behalf of his company, which was forced to pay $772 million in fines, became a national bestseller.

*Le Piege Americain* featured prominently
in a Beijing bookstore, 2019

All of these events plus the secondary sanctions against China's Equipment Development Department for buying weapons from the Russian Rosoboronexport and the sanctions on Chinese oil imports from Iran connected the dots for Beijing: America's control over the global financial infrastructure and its willingness to use its law to systematically target Chinese business abroad in order to gain profits for its own companies is a real threat to China's national security. China needed to strive not only for technological independence but also for monetary independence. It was time to dust off Zhou Xiaochuan's speech and work diligently to mount a challenge to America's dollar regime, utilizing a variety of tactics, first among them the internationalization of China's own currency, the yuan or renminbi (RMB).

## Yuanification through unification

As China ponders the next phase of its rise, it faces a dilemma about the role of its currency in international affairs. China realizes that in order to diminish the role of the dollar it must create alternative payment systems and rally as many of its trading partners to agree to trade with it in non-dollar currencies. For this it must also expand the use of the yuan and bring it to par with its influence and prestige as the second largest economy. But this is going to be a long and challenging process. In the beginning of 2019, the yuan was the world's fifth-largest payment currency, third-largest trade financing currency and fifth-largest foreign exchange transaction currency. The good news for China is that its currency is on an upward trajectory from a very low baseline. Since the IMF in 2016 added the yuan to its currency basket, the Special Drawing Rights (SDR), more than 60 countries have included the yuan in their reserve currency portfolio. To demonstrate support for the yuan, the European Central Bank (ECB) shifted €500 million of its foreign reserves to the Chinese currency.[15] The bad news for China is that the yuan is still far behind the leading currencies such as the dollar and the euro. China's currency barely makes two percent of global foreign exchange reserves held by central banks. The dollar's share in comparison is 62 percent. The euro's is 20 percent.[16] China's currency still has a great deal of catching up to do to win greater international recognition and credibility.

**Table 2: Global foreign exchange reserves, 2019 (in billion $)**
**Source: IMF**

| U.S. dollars | 6,739 |
|---|---|
| Euro | 2,206 |
| Japanese yen | 572 |
| Pound sterling | 494 |
| Chinese yuan | 212 |
| Canadian dollars | 209 |
| Australian dollars | 182 |
| Swiss francs | 15 |
| Other currencies | 267 |
| Total allocated reserves | 10,901 |

Here is the crux of the matter: the key to the internationalization of the yuan lies in market acceptance, but central banks, while slowly losing their for appetite additional exposure to the dollar, are leery about adopting the Chinese currency as an alternative. A reserve currency with Chinese characteristics is hard for them to swallow. In order for the yuan to become a tier-1 reserve currency, a few things must happen. First, it must be fully convertible to other currencies so that central bankers can exchange it at ease with other assets whenever they want. This is not the case now. China's capital controls are tight and cumbersome. Second, the Chinese government must move itself out of the exchange-rate intervention business. The CPC still feels entitled to intervene in foreign exchange markets and adjust the yuan to fit the party's economic planning. The CPC should allow full convertibility and step away from currency manipulation. It should also allow foreign enterprises to invest directly in China through yuan-denominated financial instruments and influence domestic interest rates by providing credit to China-based enterprises. But all these moves mean relinquishing some of Beijing's control over the economy, and losing control is something Beijing hates. One of China's main concerns is capital outflow. When its currency weakens, China's exports become more competitive, which is good news for many Chinese exporters. The downside is that an overly depreciated yuan could cause capital to stampede out of the country en masse, and this could lead to loss of control over the economy.

Here again Deng's advice on how to cross a river comes handy. As China becomes integrated in world affairs, particularly as the BRI develops, the first element in its yuanization strategy will be the shifting of trade with as many of its main trading partners from dollars to yuans. Since 2015, when the Russian central bank included the yuan in the list of currencies that can be accepted as reserves, China has signed several agreements with its trading partners, including Kazakhstan, South Africa, and India to conduct trade in respective currencies. Hence, trade between Russia and China is nearly 20 percent de-dollarized compared to 7 percent in 2013.[17]

A major push for yuan adoption as reserve currency and trading currency is also taking place in Africa. Today, China's population is roughly equivalent to Africa's 1.3 billion. But by the middle of the century, absent a pandemic, major war, massive uptake of birth control, or some other big surprise, Africa will account for one half of the world's population growth while China's population is projected to decline. Seven of the top twenty most populated countries of the world are projected to be in Africa: Nigeria, Democratic Republic of Congo, Ethiopia, Egypt, Tanzania, Uganda and Kenya. Currently, only four are on the list. And in March 2018, 44 African countries signed the African Continental Free Trade Agreement (AfCFTA), the single largest free trade agreement realized since the coming together of the World Trade Organization. From China's perspective, Africa is where the future lies, and the continent is the prime target for the internationalization of the yuan. For years the dollar has served as a second currency in most African countries, a hedge against weakness and volatility of the domestic currencies. But over the past several years, many African countries have introduced strict rules limiting the use of American currency.[18] This opened the door for other currencies to seize a share of foreign reserves. The yuan is playing a growing role in China's loans and enhanced trading with the continent. While in the past Chinese loans to African countries were billed in dollars, now they are increasingly billed in yuans. Central banks of African countries like Angola, Zimbabwe and Nigeria have already adopted the yuan as a reserve currency. In fact, Nigeria, which is Africa's biggest economy, has nearly 10 percent of its reserves in yuans. Other African countries like Kenya, Botswana, Burundi, Lesotho, Malawi, Mozambique, Namibia, Rwanda, Swaziland, Tanzania, Uganda and Zambia are thinking of following suit.[19] "The general conclusion is that we should use the yuan more because its time has come. We are doing more business with China so it's natural that we use the currency of the country with which we are trading," said the executive director of the Macroeconomic and Financial Management Institute of Eastern and Southern Africa (MEFMI) Caleb Fundanga.[20] For Africa, yuan adoption also makes sense for closing the widening trade deficit with China. African countries now trade more with China than with the West, and they prefer to finance their trade with yuans rather than U.S. dollars. In May 2018, government officials from 14 African nations, mostly from BRI countries in eastern and southern Africa, met in Zimbabwe to discuss the role of the yuan in international settlements, investment and foreign exchange trading. Additional progress was achieved a few months later in September 2018 when 50 African heads of government attended the Beijing

Forum on China-Africa Cooperation. The United States, on the other hand, has almost given up on Africa. The U.S. Africa Strategy launched by the Trump administration in December 2018 was weak on aid to the struggling region, especially since the administration had cut development assistance by 30 percent. Instead, it focused on counter-terrorism and on spreading fears about China's expansion into the continent. It challenged African governments to choose the United States over China for their commercial and security relationships. Africa was not impressed.

Beyond Africa, China has its sights set on another important region for yuan adoption. ASEAN, the Association of Southeast Asian Nations, is for China what Central America is for the United States—a backyard—except that ASEAN is more populated and has much greater potential for economic growth. The population of the ten countries of ASEAN surpasses 600 million. If ASEAN were a country it would be the world's most populous after China and India. Most ASEAN countries have wealthy and politically influential Chinese communities. In short, ASEAN is fertile ground for China's yuanization strategy. China has already signed agreements with several ASEAN countries to advance the use of the yuan. In 2018, for example, 13 Philippine banks, together with Bank of China, launched a trading community to make transacting using the Chinese currency cheaper and easier. Manila's Finance Secretary Carlos Dominguez said the Philippine Yuan Trading Community could reduce the cost of doing business by up to 3 percent compared to dollar transactions.[21] The yuan is also poised to replace the dollar as emergency currency for the ASEAN community. In 2000, after the traumatic Asian currency crisis, ASEAN countries formed the Chiang Mai Initiative, an IMF-style regional currency swap safety net that enables countries to access a pool of dollars in the event they need to prop up their currency. Currency swaps allow governments and businesses to bilaterally directly convert their currencies, negating the need to use dollar invoicing as the intermediary. Currently, there are about $240 billion in the Chiang Mai Initiative pool. China believes that since most of ASEAN's trade is not with the United States but rather with Asian partners like China, Japan and South Korea, the dollar should no longer be the dominant currency in the pool. In April 2019, it began to lobby ASEAN to include the yuan and the yen in the currency pool with the goal of crowding out the dollar.[22] Beyond ASEAN and Africa, since 2011, China has engaged with its other trading partners to advance direct mutual exchange of their currencies. Over the years, it has signed swap agreements with nearly 40 countries including Japan, Belarus, Brazil, Indonesia, Malaysia, Thailand, Uzbekistan, Singapore, South Korea, United Kingdom and Argentina. The amount of money swapped is growing by leaps and bounds and, with it, the demand for yuans.

A Bangkok billboard promoting yuan use in Thailand

Barter deals are another important tactic. Chinese SOEs dealing with developing countries are often deployed by Beijing to advance the cause of yuanization. Here it how it works: Country A sells copper to a Chinese company X. At the same time country A also wants to build a power station, the exact expertise of Chinese company Y. Under normal business practices, country A would have to sell the copper to company X in dollars. This means company X would have to convert yuans into dollars in order to pay for the copper. Doing so it would incur various conversion and banking costs. The money country A just earned in exchange for its copper would now be used to pay Company Y for its work on the power plant. But company Y needs yuans, not dollars. The salaries it pays to its workers are all in yuans and so are the payments for materials and components it buys mostly in China. Company Y will therefore have to convert the dollars to yuans. Here too the same currency conversion costs would apply. Under the current arrangement, all the parties lose a bit; the only winner is the U.S. government, which happens to be a minor party to the transaction only because it provides the currency enabling the transaction (and as noted earlier all the parties to the transaction are therefore exposed to the scrutiny of the U.S. Department of Justice). A better system would be for country A not to receive payment in dollars for its copper. Instead, it would receive yuan credit to cover the construction of the power plant. Through the good offices of the CPC, company X would simply credit company Y, and it would do so in yuans. This way no dollars would be involved in the entire transaction, there would be no conversion fees and the Department of Justice would have no legal grounds to prosecute the parties if U.S. law was violated. Everybody wins, except the U.S. The Chinese are highly interested in this model, which offers not only financial independence and advancement of the internationalization of the yuan but also more optimized use of funds. The savings on exchange rate fees would allow Chinese companies to offer country A and others more competitive terms.

The final tactic deployed by the CPC is the redenomination of emerging market debt. Central bankers are risk averse and their main goal is to hold reserve assets of countries that are most stable. All equal they will always prefer to buy bonds of stable economies like the U.S. or Germany over China. But for many of the BRI countries, the calculations are more complex. These countries are not only already heavily indebted to China, they also suffer from a low sovereign credit rating which makes their borrowing expensive, if not prohibitive. Of the 68 BRI countries, at least 20 have credit ratings of B and lower according to Standard & Poor. Eight BRI countries—Djibouti, Kyrgyzstan, Laos, Maldives, Mongolia, Montenegro, Pakistan and Tajikistan—are facing near-term debt distress, according to a report by the Center for Global Development.[23] These countries could be persuaded by China to redenominate their dollar debt into yuan and, in so doing, increase their exposure to the Chinese currency. In total, since 2000, China has provided almost a trillion dollars of debt to emerging markets. In its negotiations with its debtors, China will try to shift as much of this trillion dollars to its own currency.

These yuanization tactics are necessary yet not sufficient conditions for the Chinese currency to gain international prominence. Going forward, we see the yuan's portion of global reserve currency growing at a steady pace but mainly in the parts of the world where the dollar is not entrenched and where China shares substantial bilateral trade. But this may not be enough for the yuan to turn into a tier-1 reserve currency. China may be talking a good game on liberalization of its currency, but to date its actions have not met the rhetoric. In fact, even Hong Kong, which is de facto part of China, still pegs its currency, the Hong Kong dollar, to the greenback. If Beijing cannot convince its own special administrative region to accept the yuan en masse how could it convince other countries to do so? For now, the government's levers are still intact, and it will continue to determine how much yuan can be used, where it is invested and for what purposes. To strip the dollar of its strategic status, China will need to exploit other vulnerabilities, using its size and market power to advance structural changes in some of the mechanisms that give the dollar its strength. One of them is the oil market.

# 4 AS GOOD AS GOLD: FROM PETRODOLLAR TO PETROYUAN

> It is absurd that Europe pays for 80 percent of its energy import bill—with 300 billion euro a year—in U.S. dollars when only roughly 2 percent of our energy imports come from the United States. It is absurd, ridiculous that European companies buy European planes in dollars instead of euro. This all needs to be changed.
> *President of the European Commission Jean-Claude Juncker, September 2018*[1]

Oil is by far the world's most strategic commodity. This is not because it is the most voluminous commodity traded or because its market by value trumps any other commodity. It is simply because there is no major substitute in the global transportation sector. Most cars, trucks, ships and planes are made to run on nothing but petroleum fuels, leaving no possibility for healthy competition to take place. In a way, oil is to cars what the dollar is to banks. As we argued in our previous books, this is not an unsolvable problem. A spectrum of readily available technologies both on the fuel and vehicle sides can open cars to run on a variety of fuels made from a variety of energy commodities—natural gas, coal, biomass and electricity made from various sources—and hence break oil's virtual monopoly over the transportation sector.[2] But while this effort is already underway—most impressively in China—and more and more cars can be seen on the road powered by non-petroleum fuels, humanity is still beholden to oil and those who pump it, transport it and refine it. Oil and natural gas are extracted in about 100 countries, but most are insignificant players in the gigantic global energy market. Nearly half of the 90 million barrels of crude produced every day in the world originate from six countries: Russia, Saudi Arabia, Iran, Iraq, China and United States, only the last one being a real democracy. The other major producers like Nigeria, Angola, United Arab Emirates, Kuwait and Venezuela are either corrupt or dictatorial or both. The most important fact one needs to know about the global oil market is that it is a market controlled by governments—not free enterprise. The reason we must keep a watchful eye on the changes in this market is not only because it involves most of America's rivals and competitors but also because it is the first line of defense for the dollar's status as reserve currency. It is the outer wall of the castle. If breached, the inner walls will come down more easily. De-dollarization of the oil market will pave the way for the de-dollarization of the entire global commodity market—copper, coffee, wheat, lithium, pork bellies and so forth. The commodity market, estimated at $5 trillion a year, of which roughly $3 trillion is comprised of energy and minerals and the other $2 trillion is food and agricultural commodities, is a bellwether indicating the future of the dollar. Up until recently, most of the transactions in this market have been settled in dollars. But here too things are changing. Because most of the dollar insurgents are major hydrocarbon producers, they can collectively change the architecture of the oil and gas market. And this is exactly what they are doing. Most of the major energy exporters, spearheaded by Russia and Iran, as well as several major importers, most notably China, India and the

EU, have already incorporated energy in their de-dollarization strategies, shifting growing portions of their energy trading away from the greenback. The EU's annual energy import bill alone averaged $350 billion in the last five years, with roughly 80 percent of it cleared in dollars. Brussels is now convinced that this exposure to the dollar regime poses uncertainties, risks and costs that may be mitigated through a larger use of non-dollar contracts. In an April 2019 speech, Claudio Borio, head of the Monetary and Economic Department at the Bank of International Settlements encouraged this policy, arguing that "trading and settling oil in the euro would move payments from dollars to euros and thereby shift ultimate settlement to the euro's TARGET2 system. This could limit the reach of U.S. foreign policy insofar as it leverages dollar payments."[3] (TARGET 2 is the settlement system European central banks and commercial banks use to settle monetary transactions.) Imagine that Europe, China, India, Russia and a few other major players in the energy sector shifted say half of their oil trade from the dollar and whoops—a quarter of a trillion dollars no longer has something to attach itself to. But before we entertain this scenario we should go back in time to the genesis of the relations between oil and the greenback.

## The buck-barrel-bomber nexus

The marriage of oil and the dollar—the petrodollar—goes back to a 1975 agreement between the Nixon administration and the House of Saud, an agreement that proved to be one of the most consequential in modern history. During the late 1960s and early 1970s, the United States was running substantial deficits caused by the Vietnam War and the Johnson administration's Great Society-related spending. These deficits grew even bigger thanks to the oil price hike resulting from the 1973 Oil Embargo. Three years before the agreement with the Saudis, the Nixon administration was already in the middle of a process of decoupling the dollar from the international gold standard, which governed world finance since Bretton Woods. To justify his controversial August 1971 order to suspend the dollar's convertibility into gold, Nixon pegged the blame on the "attacks of international money speculators."[4] These nefarious "speculators" were not some shady Russian oligarchs or Chinese banks but none other than the French, who earlier that month had sent a warship to New York Harbor with instructions to bring back $200 million worth of French gold reserves stored at the New York Federal Reserve Bank, as well as the governments of United Kingdom, Belgium and the Netherlands who demanded the U.S. buy back hundreds of billions of dollars of foreign exchange. Just like today's dollar insurgents, those of the 1970s were quite fed up with America's exorbitant privilege and with what they viewed as the unfair advantage Americans enjoy due to the privilege of holding the world's reserve currency at the expense of other nations. In any event, Nixon's decision to decouple the dollar from gold, which is known today as the "Nixon shock," deeply troubled the oil exporters who had until then backed their oil trading with gold. Under the agreement reached in 1975 between then Secretary of State Henry Kissinger and the Saudis, any country that sought to purchase oil from the Oil Kingdom would be required to do so in dollars and in dollars alone. In exchange for Saudi Arabia's willingness to denominate its oil sales exclusively in dollars, the United States offered the vulnerable Saudis long-term security guarantees which includes protection of their oil fields. This commitment to shield the House of Saud from foreign and internal adversaries has been put to the test many times over the years - from the 1979 attack on the Grand Mosque in Mecca, through Saddam Hussein's 1990 invasion of Kuwait, to the recent rise of Iran as an existential nuclear threat to Saudi Arabia. Until 2003, tens of thousands of U.S. combat troops equipped with top-of-the-line missiles and aircraft were actually stationed in Saudi Arabia. Thanks to Saudi loyalty to what could be described as the buck-barrel-bomber nexus, by 1975 all the other members of the Organization of Petroleum Exporting Countries (OPEC) also agreed to trade their oil in dollars. This arrangement allowed OPEC members to plough their surplus dollars back into the U.S. economy through investments and the purchase of U.S. Treasuries which, in turn, allowed the U.S. government, then facing declining GNP and soaring unemployment, to finance its deficit and bolster its military. The buck-barrel-bomber nexus was an ingenious scheme. It essentially ensured that the demand for dollars would always grow in sync with the growth of the world economy, which is powered by oil. The perpetual demand for its currency allowed the U.S. government to continue to run loose fiscal policies, increase military spending, win the Cold War and engage in an interventionist foreign policy for the nearly half century that followed. Even better, the hegemony of the dollar over oil trading spread into other commodity markets, determining the pricing of all metals, energy and agricultural commodities—from nickel to sugar.

But after four decades of relative harmony, cracks are beginning to appear in the buck-barrel-bomber arrangement. One reason for this is that the umbrella organization with which the scheme was concocted, OPEC, is no longer unified in its views about the United States. In fact, some of its fourteen members, including Iran, Venezuela, Libya and Qatar (the latter decided in 2018 to leave the cartel) are under U.S. sanctions and/or deeply resentful of the United States for a variety of reasons. Additionally, America's relations with Saudi Arabia, the country that de facto runs OPEC, are not as amicable as they used to be. Many Americans cringe in the face of their government's deference to Saudi Arabia, which under normal circumstances would be treated as a pariah state. Indeed, Saudi Arabia has been given a sort of implicit blanket immunity by the U.S. government. Despite 15 of the 19 hijackers who attacked the United States on September 11 being Saudis, despite blatant Saudi efforts over decades to proliferate radical Sunni Islam globally and the sponsorship of terrorism worldwide by key Saudi royals, the Axis of Evil described by President George W. Bush in January 2002 included two of Saudi Arabia's challengers, but not Saudi Arabia itself. The kingdom's clandestine financial and logistical support for ISIS and other radical groups, its human rights violations, the arrest of hundreds of businessmen at the Ritz Carlton hotel in Riyadh where $100 billion was robbed by the regime without any due process, the brutal war in Yemen which brought millions to starvation, and the state-sponsored execution of Saudi journalist Jamal Khashoggi are known to all. But while Saudi Arabia's image in the eyes of the American public is in free-fall, the U.S. government and to some degree Congress are still unprepared to change the policy toward its strange "ally." To be sure, Saudi Arabia's sway over Washington is rooted in its role as a swing oil producer, which can inject additional barrels into the market to arrest prices when supply disruptions occur, as they sometimes do. American presidents understand the political danger of high gasoline prices and they know there is only one country that can come to the rescue when oil prices need to be forced down. No less important, Saudi Arabia is the number one buyer of U.S. defense and aerospace products. In 2018, Riyadh arms purchases from Washington surpassed those of Australia, UAE, Japan, South Korea and Israel combined. Time and again, the country's orders of military equipment bought it an insurance policy against America's wrath. For example, its order of $110 billion worth of arms blunted America's response to the Khashoggi murder. It was then that President Trump revealed what is really at the core of the U.S.-Saudi relations. "I don't want to hurt jobs. I don't want to lose an order like that," he said.[5] In April 2019, he vetoed a congressional bill to end U.S. support for the Saudi led war in Yemen. And a month later, he invoked a loophole in the Arms Control Export Act to circumvent the congressional ban of the sale of $8 billion worth of weapons to the Saudis and their Sunni allies.

Less known is the role of the petrodollar in the relations. The Saudis and the other major producers in the Gulf Cooperation Council (GCC)—Kuwait, Oman and UAE—are today the de facto guardians of the petrodollar system. As detailed earlier, many of the major players in the global oil market have jumped ship and are transacting growing portions of their oil in non-dollar currencies. The GCC, together responsible for one quarter of the world's oil exports, is the linchpin that holds the petrodollar system together. Should Saudi Arabia and its Sunni allies decide to abandon the dollar in oil transactions, it could trigger a cascading set of events that could change the world economy forever. Every barrel that shifts from dollar to something else means fewer dollars demanded in global trade. This will not only have implications for the strength of the dollar but also for America's borrowing ability. Collectively, the Saudis and their Gulf allies are the fifth largest holders of U.S. foreign debt after China, Japan, the UK and Brazil (Technically it is FAANG but as we established before that's not a country and regardless FAANG members are moving their money back to America.) Other than buying arms, the dollars the Saudis and their allies accumulate in exchange for their oil are partly used to buy U.S. Treasuries and equity in American corporations. In fact, in the first two years of the Trump presidency, the Saudis almost doubled their bond holdings. But if oil is no longer traded in dollars, the amount of dollars available for the oil exporters to recycle into the U.S. economy will shrink and with it their ability to rollover and beef up their purchases of U.S. debt, all this at a time the U.S. needs more underwriters for its ballooning liabilities.

How much of an impact the de-dollarization of oil trading might have on the demand for the dollar is hard to tell. At $70 a barrel, the global oil market is channeling roughly $2.5 trillion worth of transactions every year. This makes up something between 2 and 3 percent of the global economy. But wait, that's only crude. The market is much bigger if one includes the trade in natural gas as well as oil products—gasoline, diesel, aviation fuel, etc. A barrel of oil can be shipped from Saudi Arabia to China at a price of $70. But this barrel then generates additional economic value, much of it denominated in dollars, when it is refined into various products that are then sold around the world. Trading in derivatives such as oil futures and options is mostly dollar denominated and the nominal value of this market alone was about $5 trillion in 2018. Draining the world economy of numerous dollar transactions could not bode well for the greenback. The Saudis are aware of that. Americans less so.

Will the Saudis and their Sunni allies remain loyal to the buck-barrel-bomber system? If so, for how long? Hard to tell. Because of fracking, the United States needs to buy less oil from the Persian Gulf than previously, but China is increasingly dependent on the Sunni oil states. In fact, Saudi Arabia is already its number one oil supplier, and in 2017 China bought a stake in Abu Dhabi's National Oil Company (ADNOC). Saudi Arabia has already accepted payments in yuan for some of the oil it sends to China.[6] It also invests heavily in China's refining and petrochemical sector in order to ensure that China's refineries are technically well suited to process its high sulfur Arabian crude. While those steps are meant to appease Beijing and secure market share in China, they are also meant to send constant reminders to Washington about the importance of Saudi Arabia to America's financial supremacy. The Saudis have not been subtle about their willingness to use economic weapons against the United States. In 2016, for example, they threatened the Obama administration that they would dump U.S. Treasuries if Congress decided to pass a bill implicating the Kingdom in the September 11 attacks.[7] Three years later, the Saudis indicated to the Trump administration their intention to ditch the petrodollar and to shift their oil trading away from the dollar over Congress' attempt to pass a bill known as NOPEC, or the No Oil Producing and Exporting Cartels Act, which aimed to remove OPEC members' sovereign immunity from U.S. antitrust law. If passed, the law could have allowed OPEC members to be sued for colluding in raising oil prices.[8] For now these are only threats. The Persian Gulf countries are not likely to drop the dollar any time soon. They have good reasons not to challenge the system that has kept them safe for so long.

Other than the growing regional insecurity, which necessitates America's military umbrella, there is the sticky issue of the tight connection between the dollar and their own currencies. One Saudi riyal or one UAE dirham is always worth 27 cents; 1,000 Iraqi dinars are always worth 84 cents; and one Kuwaiti dinar is always equal to $3.30. Unlike in Russia, whose ruble is free-floating, the Gulf oil countries peg their currency to the dollar, and this protects them domestically from sharp drops in oil prices. In Saudi Arabia, where people do not pay income tax yet expect to receive cradle-to-grave social services from the government, low oil prices are a nightmare. Shifting their oil trade from the dollar to other currencies could have destabilizing implications for their domestic economies which are difficult to predict. In a region that requires economic stability to keep the masses from storming the palaces, the appetite for financial adventurism is never strong. But as usual, things again boil down to China.

## Enter the petro-yuan

For decades, the United States was the world's number one oil importer. This presented many challenges and vulnerabilities. No wonder America was elated when the scope of its shale oil reserves became apparent. Due to advanced fracking technologies, within ten years, U.S. oil Import dependency fell from roughly half to roughly a quarter of its domestic needs, and in 2016 the United States gladly handed over the title of top importer to China, whose crude oil imports have nearly doubled since 2010. Being the number one buyer of anything comes with privileges. With its buying power, China can reshape the market and set new rules, especially when oil exporters are suffering from a middling price environment and are desperate to protect market share. China imports close to 10 million barrels a day. At current prices this amounts to an annual bill of, give or take, $250 billion. Because China has a large trade surplus with the United States, it has sufficient dollars to pay for its oil imports as well as the many other commodities it relies on. But things are changing. Washington's efforts to shave off much of its trade deficit with China could mean eroding China's mountain of spare dollars which in turn means less and less of an incentive to pay for the oil in dollars. Additionally, China sees the de-dollarization of commodity trading as yet another mechanism to advance the internationalization of the yuan. For China, the disengagement from the dollar is not only a way to challenge the United States but a matter of food and energy security. China was traumatized during the global financial crisis when it realized that it had lost control over its most essential imports—oil, grains and other raw materials—primarily because everything was settled in dollars. This became a powerful driver behind the CPC's thinking about de-dollarization.

There is another incentive. Both importers and exporters pay a hefty premium for trading oil in dollars. When Kazakhstan sells oil in dollars to its neighbor China, both countries lose on the transaction. Kazakhstan receives dollars that it needs to convert to tenge, the local currency, while China has to convert yuans for dollars in order to pay Kazakhstan for its oil. Piled up over many years, these exchange rate fees are costing the two countries billions. But what if instead the two countries traded the oil in their local currencies? In this case China could pay Kazakhstan in yuans, which the Kazakhs would use to buy Chinese goods. This way no dollars are involved in the transaction. This is exactly what is happening. China is working hard to convince its oil suppliers to accept yuans either as direct payments or as part of the kind of barter deals described in the previous chapter. As it happens, many of the BRI countries are rich in natural resources, yet poor in infrastructure. China builds them roads, bridges and pipelines and in return they supply it with oil and other minerals. If the United States has a barrels-for-bombs strategy, China has a barrels-for-bridges one. In the coming years China will have a new opportunity to expand its barrels-for-bridges program and in the process deepen its presence in the Middle East while eroding the status of the dollar. This will unfold as, one by one, the war-torn countries of the region emerge from their civil wars. The civil war in Syria is already in its final stages. Syrian President Bashar Assad, with the help of Russia, is cracking down on the remaining pockets of opposition, and it is now widely assumed that he will emerge victorious from the country's nine-year civil war. The conflict in Libya is likely to be resolved sometime in the next couple of years after national elections take place. Yemen too could see the end of its civil war if the U.S. and Saudi Arabia succeed in ending Iran's destabilizing influence in the country as part of the Trump administration's broader Iran policy. With Iran's regional influence contained, Iraq too will become more conducive to national rejuvenation. As countries rise from the ashes, they will have to embark on a rapid and efficient reconstruction effort, including the rebuilding of entire national infrastructures. Countries embroiled in conflict inevitably need a large amount of capacity building support once the war is over, as well as financing for humanitarian purposes and reconstruction. Due to the length of the war, the degree of the devastation and the damage to civil society and functioning institutions, the effort to rebuild the Middle East will be extremely challenging and costly. It will be the largest reconstruction effort since the reconstruction of Europe after the Second World War. To understand the scale of investment needed: the Marshall Plan cost about $100 billion in today's dollars. Syria's reconstruction alone will require $200-$300 billion. Iraq needs nearly $90 billion to rebuild after years of war with ISIS. Libya will need at least $100 billion, and Yemen will need almost $50 billion. Altogether, the cost of the reconstruction of the Middle East could easily surpass half a trillion dollars. This effort will require significant resources, financial management and an orderly and transparent bidding process. Because all civil war countries discussed are oil economies that, before the war started, earned between 35 and 90 percent of government revenues from oil, an efficient mechanism is needed to convert oil revenues into capital dedicated to the reconstruction effort. Indeed, oil is the main source of hard currency these countries will initially own to finance their reconstruction. This presents a unique opportunity for China to barter the oil it needs for the surpluses it has in manufacturing and infrastructure building capacity. If it is up to Beijing, the dollar will have no role in this exchange.

China's efforts to avoid dollar use in energy trading are augmented by a parallel effort to de-dollarize energy pricing. Today, most of the world's hydrocarbons are not only traded in dollars but are also priced in dollars. The three main benchmarks for oil pricing: Brent, West Texas Intermediate (WTI) and Dubai/Oman, as well as the benchmark for gas, Henry Hub—named after the hub of natural gas pipelines located in Louisiana that serves as the official delivery location for futures contracts on the New York Mercantile Exchange (NYMEX) -- are all dollar denominated. This arrangement is the vestige of a period in which the Atlantic countries were the biggest market for oil. But today, the market is shifting eastward. Most of the growth in energy demand is in Asia-Pacific, yet Asia pays for its energy in dollar prices determined in Texas, Louisiana, London or Dubai. Why is that a problem? For starters, the value of the dollar is determined by the Fed's policies for considerations that are mostly domestic. Why should the quarrels between President Trump and Fed Chairman Powell over interest rates affect the price that traders in Shanghai and Singapore pay for oil? Buyers in Asia, where half the world population is based, wish to have more say about the price of the commodities they consume. While major Asian countries like Japan, South Korea, India and China are often at odds with each other, they are all in unanimous agreement that it is time for Asia to take advantage of its buying power and exercise more power over pricing. For years, OPEC has been discriminating against Asian refiners by charging them what is known as the 'Asian oil premium.' This premium has its origins in the late 1980s when OPEC decided to adopt separate maker-based prices for its three main markets: Brent for Europe, WTI for the U.S. and Dubai/Oman for Asia. The Asian market was offered higher prices - by an average of $1-$1.50 a barrel - than the other two, and Asian buyers, who lacked collective bargaining power, were essentially price takers. In other words, when Saudi Aramco directs its oil westward, it sells it for one price based on Brent. The official selling price of the same exact oil is priced according to the Oman crude futures traded on the Dubai Mercantile Exchange when heading east. Not fair. But times have changed and with Asian buyers dominating the market, there is no reason they should agree to be squeezed. And, indeed, the premium is being gradually eliminated. But the Asians want more than just equality. They want to leverage their buying power and determine the price in Asia itself. This requires the formation of a widely accepted regional trading hub for oil and gas with a futures exchange and sufficient storage facilities to clear the transactions. To date, it has been impossible for Asians to reach a consensus about the location of such a hub. While China is the largest and fastest growing Asian market, the other Asian players are reluctant to accept it as a regional price maker. This is partly due to traditional aversion to the idea of China becoming a regional hegemon and partly due to China's underdeveloped financial markets, lack of transparency and deep government influence over the economy, especially its Big Three oil giants—Sinopec, China National Petroleum Corporation

(CNPC) and China National Offshore Oil Corporation (CNOOC). On the flip side, China, which sees itself as the leader of Asia is not likely to agree that such a hub be hosted in Japan, South Korea or Singapore. Beijing knows that no real Asian market can succeed without its participation. The result is a stalemate in which everyone loses.

With or without the support of the rest of Asia, China is now trying to claim pricing power through a new instrument, a futures contract, called petro-yuan. The first time China issued a domestic oil futures contract was in 1993. But the experiment came to an abrupt end due to extreme price fluctuation and bad execution. Other efforts followed, none with greater success. Eventually, in 2014, after much study and improvement, the China Securities Regulatory Commission approved the launch of a yuan denominated oil futures contract. This new contract actually came close to entering the market in 2015, but a crash in the Chinese stock market that summer temporarily stalled the project. Finally, on March 26, 2018, the first trades in crude oil futures denominated in yuan, commonly referred to as petro-yuan, appeared on the screens of the Shanghai International Energy Exchange. Initially the new benchmark faced great skepticism. In 2006, India introduced crude oil futures denominated in rupees. Ten years later, Russia tried something similar. In both cases the results were underwhelming. This is not surprising. The oil industry is notoriously risk-averse and traders are creatures of habit. Why would China's petro-yuan fare better? The simple reason for China's optimism is the vastness of the Chinese market and the growth in demand for energy. Already the world's number one oil importer, China's oil demand is expected to rise by 30 percent by 2040. It is also on track to become the largest consumer of Liquefied Natural Gas (LNG) as it implements policies to reduce its coal use. To boost support for the petro-yuan, the Chinese government is increasingly forcing state-owned companies to purchase oil using the new contracts. It also plans to condition foreign access to the Chinese crude market on a requirement to benchmark some volumes against the Shanghai price. Furthermore, oil is just the first commodity to be traded in yuans. Following it will soon come rubber and metals like copper, aluminum, zinc and lead.

If one is to judge from the first year of trading in petro-yuan, the results are quite promising. Within one year, it gobbled a 6 percent market share of the incumbent benchmark, registering turnover of $2.48 trillion.[9] To compare, twenty years ago when Brent futures contracts started trading, Brent in the first year took a 3.1 percent share from the then-dominant WTI contract.[10] But petro-yuan acceptance has been limited to the Chinese market. What happens outside of China will have much to do with the conduct of Beijing and especially its response to the deepening tension with the United States. To boost the petro-yuan, Beijing could compel its energy-rich neighbors like Turkmenistan, Kazakhstan and of course Russia to shift their trading to petro-yuan. Isolated countries like Iran and Venezuela will also welcome the option of trading oil in yuans, especially if this translates to political and economic support. China could also use the infrastructure projects of the Belt and Road Initiative—deepwater ports, oil and gas terminals, transnational pipelines and rail links—to build support for the petro-yuan. The bigger unknown is the petro-yuan's acceptance in the GCC and the Asia-Pacific region, China's own backyard. In the Middle East, trading oil in yuan is a welcome idea. In fact, a plan to issue contracts denominated in yuan was part of the agenda in the China-Saudi Economic Forum, but as explained before, unless a fundamental shift occurs in Saudi-U.S. relations, Riyadh and its allies will be extremely careful not to show too much enthusiasm for any new mechanism that might undermine the dollar. As for the Asia-Pacific region, the rise of an Asian oil benchmark could mark the tipping point in an ongoing process of economic integration, but full acceptance of this benchmark will take a great deal of coaxing and diplomatic effort by Beijing. Just like the challenge of increasing market acceptance of the yuan itself, winning support for the yuan-based oil futures will require China to address issues like lack of market data, fears of currency manipulation by Chinese authorities and the incestuous relations between the CPC, its oil companies and the state banks financing them.

## The dark side of oil trading

The efforts by major energy trading governments to de-dollarize the oil market are not occurring in a vacuum. Another group of market players share the same interest. To understand why, one needs to better understand the mechanics of the oil trading business. In most oil exporting countries, decisions on pricing and production levels are made by National Oil Companies (NOC) which are closely controlled by their governments. If you thought the word's oil is controlled by publicly owned multinational oil companies like Exxon, Chevron and BP, think again. NOCs own 85 percent of the world's proven conventional oil reserves and roughly three quarters of global production. The multinationals have good brand recognition, but they are far from being market movers. They are pure price takers. NOCs pump oil, sell it and direct most of the revenues to their governments' coffers. The government, for its part, uses the money as it sees fit to provide social services, build roads, maintain armed forces and in some cases invest or save some of it for a rainy day through a sovereign wealth fund. Some NOCs award licenses to foreign companies to jointly produce the oil. This arrangement is known as a production sharing agreement. The foreign company brings the knowhow and does most of the work while the NOC mostly provides physical and regulatory protection for the enterprise. The agreed upon portion of the oil proceeds, typically more than 50 percent, is recycled back into the NOC. In other cases, the NOC invites foreign companies to bid for concessions to develop oil fields and produce the oil all by themselves. Often the decisions on granting oil concessions are not open for bidding. The awarding of exploration and production rights can be an incredibly corrupt practice in which the tenders are tailored to specific bidders in a non-transparent way.[11]

The pricing and sale of the crude by the NOCs is equally shady. Typically, the price of oil is based on one of the widely used international benchmarks mentioned before: Brent, WTI, etc. But in reality, nobody trading with NOCs really pays the benchmark prices. NOC executives have the discretion to offer handsome discounts. For example, if Brent stands at $70/barrel, the NOC may offer the buyer a $10/barrel discount on the Brent price. Why would the NOC offer the oil below market price? In some cases, this has a legitimate reason. A country under international sanctions yet desperate for income, think Iran or Venezuela, may want to secure market share in an importing country and for this it is willing to forego some of its profits. In other cases, the discount may be offered to compensate for political risk. All equal, buyers will always prefer to buy their oil from stable sources like Norway or the United States. Unstable countries like Libya, Iraq or Yemen that want to maintain their market share must make the deal significantly sweeter for the buyer. But often discounts have a more nefarious reason. NOC executives, typically with the blessing of government officials who oversee them, offer traders handsome discounts with an understanding that some of the discount will be recycled back to them in the form of kickbacks. Countless billions of oil revenues are being denied to the people of oil exporting countries each year because of this practice. Money that could otherwise be used for education, health and infrastructure is lining the pockets of corrupt government officials, military leaders and other members of the exporting countries' elites. This creates a vicious cycle. Once the ruling elite has access to independent sources of income, it can more easily tighten its grip on power, fuel conflict and oppress any emerging opposition. With this absolute power, they can steal and misuse even more of the country's resources. The corruption is not limited to the sellers' side. Often the buyers too are non-transparent state enterprises. In China, the world's number one crude importer, most oil imports are contracted by the big three major state-run oil companies. Executives of those companies who are authorized to source oil from foreign NOCs hold incredible power. Many of them are politically connected to the state apparatus and are quite susceptible to graft. Decisions to source crude from one supplier or another would often depend on the personal benefits they can secure. In recent years, the Chinese government has not only cracked down on this practice, it has worked to diminish the power of the big three by granting oil import quotas to a handful of private energy firms. But those reforms still have a long way to go. In 2018, the two main private oil giants, CEFC China Energy Company and Brightoil Petroleum, got into financial problems and were charged with corruption, proving that the business culture in the private sector is not any better than that of the SOEs.

Since most of the world's energy transactions are carried out in dollars, the American currency is inadvertently the oil that lubricates a corruption machine of gigantic scale. It is therefore no coincidence that Americans are less inclined to get involved in the oil trading business. Of the world's top oil trading companies—Gunvor, Vitol, Trafigura, Glencore—not one is American. The current nature of the business, particularly the frequent dealing with government officials of unsavory countries, makes the international oil trading business almost by design a Go-to-Jail card for U.S. citizens. The reason is that under the FCPA and other international anti-corruption laws, third party intermediaries involved in facilitating oil deals may be liable for corrupt payments or other benefits provided to government officials, even if they did not facilitate the payments themselves. This means that if part of the $10 discount offered by the

NOC was somehow recycled back into the pocket of a government official, the trader could be considered to be part of a conspiracy and could potentially face legal consequences. In recent years, as part of a global pushback against international corruption and money laundering, the U.S. government has ramped up its FCPA enforcement, stretching the definitions of conspiracy and increasingly casting its net to target individuals—not only corporations. The United States is not alone in this. The Bribery Act in the UK, for example, has even wider reach than the FCPA. This implies that the legal risk of partaking in energy commodity trading involving foreign governments has become too high. But while Americans and Brits are being crowded out of the industry, there are always enough foreigners who are eager to be part of the multi-billion dollar energy trading business, even in the face of a growing risk of U.S. extraterritorial prosecution. For them, especially those dealing with countries and companies under U.S. sanctions, the only way to work around the long arm of U.S. authorities is to stay clear of dollar denominated transactions and of U.S.-based banks.

# 5 ANOTHER BRICS IN THE WALL

> The most dangerous threat to America would be
> a grand coalition of China and Russia, united not
> by ideology, but by complementary grievance.
> *Former National Security Advisor Zbigniew Brzezinski, 2017*

In previous chapters we outlined the motivations of the international insurgency against the dollar's reserve currency status. We also covered some of the tactics deployed so far, arguing that the growing number of players who make the de-dollarization bloc have created a bandwagon effect which entices more and more players resentful of Washington's conduct to join and reinforce the movement. But anti-American sentiment, strong as it may be, is not enough for de-dollarization to gain the serious momentum needed to challenge the dollar reserve currency status. For this to happen there must be a more formal consensus backed by an organizational structure and coordination mechanism, similar to the one that gave rise to our current multinational monetary and exchange rate system in the first place.

While the dollar began its ascendance in the 1920s, right after World War I, it was only two decades later, in July 1944, that it was officially crowned as the alternative to the Sterling as the world's reserve currency. World War II was still raging, but in that summer of 1944 it was clear that the allies' path to victory was no longer reversible. The landing in Normandy was declared a success, Rome was liberated, Paris was within reach, and in the east the Japanese were evicted from Burma. It was time to sit down to discuss what the post-war global economic order should look like. For three full weeks, hundreds of policymakers and economists from 44 countries gathered in Bretton Woods, New Hampshire for a monetary and financial conference to lay the foundations for what became the new world financial system. Under the agreement that was reached, all currencies were to be pegged to gold (i.e., gold standard), and the U.S. dollar was officially recognized as the world's reserve currency. It too was linked to the price of gold with a fixed exchange rate of $35/ounce. Additionally, the summit gave rise to two important multilateral institutions which serve us to this day: the International Monetary Fund (IMF) to monitor exchange rates and to lend money to needy nations and the World Bank, which was formed to provide financial assistance for post-war reconstruction and is today the most important development bank. Numerous books and articles have been written about the intense negotiations in Bretton Woods and the various dilemmas the delegates faced. In the end, what enabled the creation of such a broad international consensus was the collective realization that Britain had ended its historical role as the world's superpower, and it was time to pass the baton to the United States. After all, it was the Americans who were bankrolling both the allied war effort and the reconstruction effort that was about to ensue.

Today's de-dollarization movement still lacks broad international consensus, a sense of urgency or multilateral mechanisms that could support a Bretton Woods-style architecture. Presently what we have is a loose and largely uncoordinated coalition of actors who may share a similar agenda and some rudimentary instruments to work with but no collective bargaining powers, no organization, no leadership, and none of the game changing technologies needed to offer central bankers throughout the world an alternative to the dollar, one that is not only safe, stable and fully liquid but also one that redefines their expectations, allowing them to benefit from functionalities not offered by today's dollar system. Equally important, it lacks the trust of the fence-sitting countries which may have reservations about the future of the dollar but are under no illusions the alternative is any better. What the movement *does* have is the conviction that the United States has reached its peak, that decline is unavoidable, that emerging markets should be better represented in global institutions and that the creation of an alternative monetary system is due. What this system will look like and how it will be governed are still unanswered questions. But as the anti-dollar coalition continues to coalesce, its members are slowly gravitating toward a common vision.

### China and Russia: Two-power standard

The single most important prerequisite for upending the dollar system is critical mass. In other words, there must be sufficient economic firepower to back up the alternative system and build on it. In today's world, such critical mass can only be anchored by the combined economic and geopolitical powers of the two main revisionist powers - China and Russia. The two neighbors have never shared great love for each other, and to this day they harbor suspicions about each other's strategic plans to gain influence over the former Soviet Union territories and beyond. But those suspicions are outweighed by a shared anxiety about America's surrounding of both with military bases and warships as well as a common desire to repel the United States from what they perceive to be their respective spheres of influence, Eastern Europe and parts of the Middle East in Russia's case and Southeast Asia and the South China Sea in China's. When it comes to Northeast Asia, both countries harbor historic grievances toward Japan, and they both see eye-to-eye on the future of the Korean Peninsula. While they are both uncomfortable with North Korea's nuclear ambitions, they abhor even more the idea of an American foothold north of the 38th parallel.

For all their differences, the two countries complement each other in more than one way. Russia has vast land, wealth of natural resources, including gigantic oil and gas reserves but it lacks what China has the most—people, money, and unparalleled industrial output capacity. Russia may have reservations about some elements of China's BRI, but on the whole it welcomes the idea of Eurasian integration through infrastructure upgrades, provided that it corresponds with the vision of its Eurasian Economic Union (EAEU) and that the corridors connecting Asia and Europe traverse Russian territory and support its design to counterbalance U.S. presence in the Middle East. To this end, the two countries have already created the Russian-Chinese Investment Bank as well as an investment fund worth some $10 billion to develop trade, economic investment, and scientific cooperation. With Europe trying to diversify its energy supply away from Russia, the Kremlin is placing high hopes on China as the main market for Russian energy. It is already the largest crude oil supplier to China and will soon become its largest natural gas supplier when the Power of Siberia pipeline starts to deliver gas from Russia's Far East to China.

Russia and China certainly present a serious challenge to U.S. military superiority. They have the two most powerful militaries after the U.S., and their combined navies are more than double the size of the U.S. Navy by number of vessels. While the U.S. is probably capable of taking on each of these military powers separately, albeit not without great pain, the thought of confronting a combined Russian-Chinese coalition should unsettle even the most bullish military planner.

When it comes to de-dollarization, the two countries share a complementary agenda. On June 6th, 2019, while Trump commemorated D-Day in Europe, Xi and Putin, leaders of two of America's World War II allies, met in St. Petersburg to upgrade their strategic relations to what was dubbed by the *Washington Post* as "an alliance for the 21st century."[1] Among the understandings the two leaders reached was a historic agreement on currency.

"Settlements and payments for goods, service and direct investments between economic entities of the Russian Federation and the People's Republic of China are made in accordance with the international practice and the legislation of the sides' states with the use of foreign currency, the Russian currency (rubles) and the Chinese currency (yuan)," the agreement said.[2]

It is not the first time in history that an incumbent power faces a challenge from a coalition of the second and third largest powers. At the end of the 19th century, Great Britain was deeply concerned about the Franco-Russian Alliance. The British adopted the "two-power standard" which compelled the Royal Navy to maintain a sea power at least equal to the combined strength of the French and Russian navies - the next two largest after the British Navy. The ensuing arms race put enormous economic strain on the British treasury, contributing to the breakout of World War I and the subsequent economic collapse of the empire. The lesson is that when facing two major challengers at once, it is always best to do anything possible to try to split them and exploit potential tensions between them—divide and rule. Driving a wedge between the Soviet Union and China and ensuring that the two Eurasian powers balanced each other was exactly Washington's policy in the 1970s. In fact, this was the main motivation behind President Nixon's decision to visit China in 1972 and to establish diplomatic relations with it. However, in recent years, since it has become apparent that China's rise may be a threat to America, both the Obama and Trump administrations failed to drive such a wedge. In fact, the exact opposite occurred. Trump's National Security Strategy, which was released in December 2017, repeatedly lumped Russia and China together, highlighting their combined challenge to American power, influence, and interests and their attempts to erode American security and prosperity.[3] The Pentagon's 2018 National Defense Strategy stated: "Long-term strategic competitions with China and Russia are the principal priorities for the Department of Defense, and require both increased and sustained investment, because of the magnitude of the threats they pose to U.S. security and prosperity today, and the potential for those threats to increase in the future."[4]

Washington's treatment of its two major rivals as two peas in a pod may prove to be one of the biggest strategic blunders in the history of the United States. It has effectively sent Russia and China into each other's arms. They share hundreds of billions of dollars' worth of joint projects and are engaged in large-scale military exercises. Putin and Xi have seen each other more frequently than any other pair of international leaders, and they seem to have warm relations. While both countries know that forging a formal alliance would not be in their interest as it might alienate India, Japan and Europe, informally they rely on each other like never before to pursue their shared vision of challenging the U.S.-centric system. The verdict of the U.S. intelligence community as presented in the January 2019 National Threat Assessment: "China and Russia are more aligned than at any point since the mid-1950s, and the relationship is likely to strengthen in the coming years as some of their interests and threat perceptions converge, particularly regarding perceived U.S. unilateralism and interventionism."[5] The combined military and economic power wielded by Russia and China could be a defining factor in their ability to usher in an alternative multinational economic bloc which will bring to bear the combined economic power of multiple countries and institutions. What will this bloc look like? A model for such a potential grouping was attempted in the past by the Soviet Union, with mixed results, and its reincarnation is being created today right before our eyes.

## From COMECON to BRICS+

The same post-World War II conditions that gave rise to Bretton Woods and the new economic world order that followed also triggered action on the other side of the Iron Curtain. In 1947, the U.S. and its war allies concluded the General Agreement on Tariffs and Trade (GATT), the precursor to today's WTO, with the goal of promoting international trade by reducing or eliminating trade barriers such as tariffs or quotas. The following year, the U.S. Congress approved the Marshall Plan for the reconstruction of Europe, and billions of dollars began to cross the Atlantic.

These initiatives alarmed the Soviet bloc. Joseph Stalin was concerned that the economic benefits offered by the Marshall Plan, the World Bank and other elements of the Western-led architecture would be too tempting for some Soviet leaning states. He had to find a way to preempt a drift of those countries toward the West by luring them into a joint economic bloc that could offer them equally attractive incentives. In short, he had to ensure they remain cut off from the Euro-American bloc. To this end, in 1949 he created the Council for Mutual Economic Assistance (COMECON). The COMECON was initially a loose coalition of five Soviet leaning countries: Bulgaria, Czechoslovakia, Hungary, Romania and, of course, the Soviet Union itself. Albania and East Germany joined shortly after followed by Mongolia, Poland, Vietnam and Cuba. After Stalin's death in 1953, the COMECON began to establish itself as a coordination mechanism for the various socialist countries' central planning efforts. In November 1962, Soviet Premier Nikita Khrushchev called for "a common single planning organ," an idea that triggered resistance among some of the members. The COMECON was not a great success story, and it ultimately fizzled out with the fall of the Soviet Union. What is relevant to our topic is the adoption in 1964 of a joint exchange currency for all COMECON members. It was called the Transferable Ruble (TR) with a vision of becoming the super national collective currency of the broader socialist world. This new backed-by-gold currency was managed by a dedicated institution called the International Bank for Economic Cooperation (IBEC). The idea behind the TR was to allow COMECON members to conduct trade between each other in a common currency. In theory this sounded like a good idea. In reality it turned out to be a flop. COMECON members clashed for years about the conversion ratio between the Soviet ruble and the TR, and its use remained limited.[6] But past failure is not going to deter today's rejectionists from repeating the experiment, this time on the basis of BRICS, the union of five major emerging economies: Brazil, Russia, India, China and South Africa. BRICS—the name was coined in 2001 by Jim O'Neill, then chief economist of Goldman Sachs—is a strange creature. It is not really a formal organization with a headquarters and president—at least not yet. It has no charter or bylaws. And yet, in some respects it has become one of the most influential groups in the world.

BRICS was first convened in July 2009 in Yekaterinburg in central Russia, and its members have been gathering annually ever since to craft a common agenda and seek a greater role in the world economy and its financial institutions. Culturally and geographically, BRICS members do not have much in common. They represent different continents, cultures and political ideologies. What they do have in common is a strong desire to be reckoned with by the existing order proportionate to their growing collective economic power. The alliance of the underrepresented if you will. Its founders have a legitimate case. The five BRICS countries represent more than 40 percent of the world's population and their combined nominal GDP is a quarter of the world's total. More importantly, they are the principal engines of global GDP growth. Combined, they contribute nearly one half of the world economic growth. This makes BRICS members an incredibly powerful subgroup within the G-20 structure. Yet, of the five, only Russia and China have seats on the UN Security Council. The world's largest democracy, India, and the largest economy of Latin America, Brazil, don't. BRICS members are also underrepresented in major international institutions like the IMF and the World Bank, and they want to change global institutions in ways that make it more advantageous to them.

One of the main principles BRICS members swear by is non-interference. BRICS leaders are in no mood to be lectured to about governance, human rights, environmental misbehavior, territorial aggression or other transgressions for which they are often criticized by the West. Instead, they want to shift the international agenda to issues closer to their heart like economic development, investment, productivity, trade and currency. As BRICS members have about $4 trillion in combined foreign exchange reserves, with the lion's share held by China, they want to have a greater say in how development money is being allocated. In 2012, BRICS pledged $75 billion to the IMF to boost its lending power. But there were strings attached. BRICS demanded a voting reform within the IMF to allow better representation for them in par with their growing weight in the global economy and contribution to global growth. In 2014, at the sixth BRICS summit in Fortaleza, Brazil, BRICS leaders went further. They decided to set up a development bank called the New Development Bank (NDB), which competes with the World Bank as a source of project financing for the developing world. Headquartered in Shanghai, the NDB concentrates on infrastructure development, energy exploration and exploitation, including clean energy. BRICS countries have also created a $100 billion Contingency Reserve Arrangement (CRA), meant to provide additional liquidity protection to member countries during balance of payments problems just like the IMF does. As they stated at the conclusion of their October 2016 summit in Goa, India, BRICS members believe that the NDB and the CRA may eventually challenge Bretton Woods' World Bank-IMF hegemony over matters such as emergency assistance, infrastructure building and post-war reconstruction.

The 2017 BRICS Summit in Xiamen, China

While within its current structure BRICS can show some important progress, there is a sense that the group is starting to encounter limits on further integration. If the group is to turn into the key organization of the post-Pax Americana world order, as China and Russia would like it to be, then the next logical step in its evolution is to focus on expansion. The first step will be the creation of what has become known as BRICS+ circle, building on the fact that BRICS is represented by one major power on virtually every continent of the developing world. China and Russia already have leadership roles in major regional integration blocs like the Shanghai Cooperation Organization (SCO), which includes

Tajikistan, Kazakhstan, Uzbekistan and Kyrgyzstan and as of recently four new members: India, Pakistan, Iran and Mongolia. BRICS founders can also draw on their relations with other groupings they influence like the South African Customs Union (SACU), Eurasian Economic Union (EAEU), South Asian Association for Regional Cooperation (SAARC), Mercado Común del Sur (Mercosur, or Southern Common Market, the South American trade bloc comprised of Argentina, Brazil, Paraguay and Uruguay), as well as the China-ASEAN FTA. If done right, the BRICS+ circle can include as many as 35 countries. Even countries not belonging to the above groupings have expressed interest in joining BRICS. One of them is Turkey. Turkish President Erdogan even suggested changing the group's name to BRICST once Turkey is admitted.[7] With 93 million people and with one of the largest markets in Africa, Egypt is also interested in joining the group.[8] Other potential new members are Bangladesh, Indonesia, Pakistan, and Jamaica.

Should this happen, BRICS+ countries could form alliances within other international organizations and thus block U.S. and European efforts from steering these organizations in ways that they believe hurt the group's members. In the IMF, for example, the United States currently maintains a 16.73 percent majority that allows it to block other countries. The consolidated share of BRICS members is just below 14 percent. But the addition of BRICS+ partners would raise the consolidated share of the vote to a point BRICS+ can have a blocking stake with respect to the key decisions of the IMF. Such upstaging of the United States is exactly what China and Russia want to achieve. A similar power shift can take place in the WTO at a time the United States and Europe are discussing ways to reform the organization in ways that may not be to the liking of Beijing and Moscow.

## The five R's

One of BRICS' top priorities is denting the hegemony of the U.S. dollar and the petrodollar in the global financial system. To this end, the group could serve as a platform for extending the use of non-dollar currencies in trade and investment transactions. The NDB is expected to be an important player in the process. To a large extent, this will be enabled by the group's holding most of the world's energy resources. Today, BRICS members control nine percent of the world's proven reserves of conventional oil and 21 percent of all global natural gas. As BRICS expands to become BRICS+, the figures will increase to 40 percent of the world's oil and 40 percent of the world's gas. With so much of the world's energy under the group's control and with some of the world's largest energy importers among its members, BRICS will be able to reshape the world's energy trading and this, as discussed in the previous chapter, could pose a serious challenge to the petrodollar system.

Shifting their internal trade to national currencies is a necessary yet insufficient step in the effort to challenge the dollar's reserve currency status. To achieve their ultimate goal, BRICS members may have to introduce a common currency as they have already begun to discuss at the 2018 BRICS summit in Johannesburg. One approach they could take is to follow the SDR model of the IMF and create a competing basket of BRICS currencies. BRICS members would certainly prefer their own basket to the SDR due to the heavy weight of the dollar in the SDR - 41 percent (the only currency of a BRICS member in the SDR is the yuan which comprises just 10 percent of the basket).

A BRICS or BRICS+ version of SDR would be based on the Five R's—the Brazilian Real, Russian Ruble, Indian Rupee, Chinese Renminbi and South African Rand. Just as in the case of SDR, all Five R's could be part of a basket whose value would be determined daily based on market exchange rates. But the problem with the SDR is that it is not really a currency but a unit of account of the IMF and some other international organizations. SDR can be used to settle debts among governments as well as between governments and the IMF itself. But this has limited use. SDR is not designed to be used by private sector players. In other words, private companies cannot just invoice their trading partners in SDR. Until markets offer an option for SDRs to be bought and sold with ease and until banks can receive SDR denominated deposits and issue SDR denominated loans, SDR use will remain limited. Another problem with the SDR is that it is not particularly attractive as a tool to enhance market liquidity in times of crisis such as was the case in 2008. Under current rules, SDR issuance requires an 85 percent majority of IMF voting power. This may not be conducive to quick action when the house is on fire. The above deficiencies of the SDR will no doubt apply to the Five R's as well. Building private markets in Five R's denominated financial instruments will require the main stakeholders to invest a great deal of effort in improving the liquidity of their markets and developing financial products that central banks and other international investors find attractive. This will be a long and agonizing process.

An even less likely scenario would be the formation of a currency union for all BRICS+ members. Twenty years after the launch of the euro, with 19 European countries going through painstaking effort to preserve their currency union, the idea of a rerun with different players is less than appealing. Why would countries that are so culturally and politically dissimilar, spread over four continents, succeed where 19 somewhat similar European countries failed? If a BRICS currency is to fare better than the euro, it must be based on the old concept of representative money rather than the highly compromised system of fiat money.

## Gold Standard 2.0 anyone?

Since its invention, money has had to fulfill two roles: it is a way to store value and it is a medium of exchange. In other words, whether it is a silver coin, an ounce of gold or a green piece of paper saying "In God We Trust" it must be acceptable to everyone, because everyone believes that it can be exchanged for something of value whether it is a pair of shoes or a movie ticket. Perhaps the biggest revolution in monetary affairs was the transition from representative money -- money that is backed typically by a precious metal like gold or silver -- to fiat money. Under a system governed by representative money, the amount of money issued to the public must always correspond to the amount of precious metals in the issuer's vault. Fiat money, on the other hand, has no inherent value. It is simply created on a whim by a central government, and it is widely used by the people simply because we are conditioned to believe that no matter what, the government, with all the powers behind it, will always guarantee its value. The transition from representative money to fiat money has accelerated in the past half century since the United States, under President Nixon, withdrew from the Gold Standard, essentially de-linking the value of the dollar from gold. The U.S. government was no longer obligated to limit its money supply. It issued more and more money in the form of dollar denominated financial instruments, and the world has always been there to absorb them. But while the United States may have opened the floodgates, it is by no means the only country to take advantage of the hollow nature of fiat currencies. The only way BRICS money can take off is if it reverses the trend from faith-based money to a value-based one. For this to happen its currency needs to be physically backed by gold as well as a new payment system to support it. In other words, BRICS would have to create a Gold Standard 2.0 where members will be able to trade, and while the road to implementation is long, there are some signs that BRICS members and their allies may already be moving in this direction.

The idea of a new currency backed by gold is not new. In the wake of the 1997 Asian financial crisis, Malaysia's Prime Minister Mahathir Mohamad promoted the idea of an Islamic Gold Dinar to become a legal tender of financial exchange in the Muslim world. The idea did not go anywhere, and Mahathir left office in 2003. But in 2018, when he came back to power as the world's oldest leader, Mahathir began to promote a new vision for a gold currency, this time a Pan-Asian alternative currency to be used among Asian countries in order to avoid the so-called "dollar trap."[9] The big question is whether BRICS countries and non-members like Malaysia and Indonesia can beef up the gold reserves in the vaults of their central banks to the level needed to back up a common currency. This would require the buildup of a gigantic amount of gold at least equivalent to the 8,133 tons presently held by the United States, the world's largest owner of gold. Currently, the official gold reserve of all five BRICS countries is just over half of that, about 4,600 tons. Long way to go. But keeping an eye on the gold market is incredibly important in this day and age. Since the sanctions on Russia were imposed, the Kremlin's central bank has been the number one gold buyer, acquiring 828 tons in just four years, bringing Russia's total reserves to over 2,000 tons. India is also building up stocks of the yellow metal.

As always, the wild card is China. China's official gold reserves have grown from 1,054 tons in mid-2015 to 1,852 tons at the end of 2018.[10] But there are reasons to believe that China's real reserves are far larger than the "official" ones, as many transactions on the Shanghai Gold Exchange are Over the Counter (OTC) and hence are not reported. On its face, China only keeps a small portion of its foreign exchange reserves, roughly two percent, in gold compared to countries like the U.S., Germany, France and Italy, where gold's share of national reserves is over 60 percent. So it makes perfect sense for China to increase its reserves especially in light of its desire to increase its credibility with the IMF and to enhance the international status of the yuan. But China's official numbers as presented to the world every several years by its State Administration of Foreign Exchange (SAFE) should be taken with a big—very big—grain of salt. The scope of its true reserves is the biggest mystery of the world economy, and the answer to this enigma could have a huge impact on its future. Various experts who keep track of China's gold market and who attempted to estimate China's actual gold reserves using different methodologies came up with figures ranging from 4,000 tons to 10,000 tons with an additional 10,000 tons held by the Chinese public.[11] In other words, it is quite probable that China owns more gold than France, Italy, Germany and perhaps even the United States. The reason experts are skeptical about China's 1,852 tons claim is that China is the number one gold producing nation (South Africa, another BRICS member, is number two) and for the most part its production - China's annual gold output is roughly 450 tons - remains in the mainland. In addition, it is widely claimed that the PBOC has been buying roughly 500 tons of gold per year since 2009 and much of the buying has been through covert operations. James Rickards describes in his book *The Death of Money* an eye witness testimony of a senior manager at security firm G4S who had participated in a secret People's Liberation Army (PLA) supported logistical operation to transport a substantial volume of gold into China via central Asia.[12] Another reason for the skepticism about China's official reserves is that, unlike in Western economies where gold is held by the central bank, it is believed that in China much of the government's gold is held outside the control of the PBOC, for example with the military and other organs of the CPC. The Chinese never keep all their eggs in one basket. In other words, we may be getting the truth about the PBOC reserves but there may be other PBOC-like deposits which hold most of China's gold.

Revealing its true gold reserves would be out of the question for the CPC as it could cause enormous disruption in the world economy. News that China has thousands of tons of unaccounted gold would send gold prices to historical highs and this would have a hugely destabilizing impact on financial markets. It would also significantly strengthen the yuan against the dollar which would severely hurt China's export oriented economy. Furthermore, the PBOC has huge dollar holdings which could lose significant value should China reveal its true gold holding. Additionally, if China comes clean about its gold holdings this would be a direct challenge to American supremacy. China is not yet ready for that. It may be in the future. Its true gold reserves may therefore be the economic equivalent of a nuclear bomb in the basement. When the secret is revealed the world economy will never be the same.

**Beyond Gold**

Gold is not the only precious metal that can support the new currency. There are other precious metals that can become reserve assets, and, as Table 3 shows, all of them are concentrated in BRICS countries. Palladium and platinum are two metals belonging to what is known as Platinum Group Metals (PGM) which in addition to the two also includes Rhodium. Unlike gold, which is mostly used as a store of value and is therefore widely recognized as a reserve asset, palladium and platinum are industrial metals and are therefore less liquid. Despite their inherent value per unit of volume, they have never been recognized by the IMF and central banks as reserve assets. Their main industrial use is in catalytic converters and diesel automobile engines. Currently, catalytic converters account for approximately half of their global demand. But the world's transportation sector is undergoing historical changes which will no doubt affect the supply and demand patterns for PGM. Due to the strategic problems associated with oil supply and the environmental problems associated with combustion engine pollution, the automotive industry is gradually shifting from petroleum-powered internal combustion engines, especially diesel engines, to alternative propulsion technologies, like batteries. If demand for battery operated vehicles gains momentum, demand for platinum and palladium in the automotive sector is likely to take a hit. However, fuel cells, the main competing technology to batteries, do require platinum. If *they* take off in a big way, it will create a new demand stream for the metal.

**Table 3: Top five producers of precious metals**

|   | Gold | Platinum | Palladium |
|---|---|---|---|
| 1 | China | South Africa | Russia |
| 2 | South Africa | Russia | South Africa |
| 3 | Australia | Zimbabwe | Canada |
| 4 | Russia | U.S. | U.S. |
| 5 | U.S. | Canada | Zimbabwe |

For the moment, these are big unknowns. What is clear is that first the reserve base of these metals is significant enough to increase production should they become more of a store of value rather than purely industrial metals. Second, BRICS countries China, Russia and South Africa, which produces roughly 90 percent of the world's platinum, are blessed with substantial reserves of these metals and as such can augment their reserve assets to back future currencies in a possible Gold Standard 2.0 architecture.

# 6  RISING PHOENIX

"Thirty years from now, Americans, Japanese, Europeans, and people in many other rich countries, and some relatively poor ones will probably be paying for their shopping with the same currency. Prices will be quoted not in dollars, yen or D-marks but in, let's say, the phoenix. The phoenix will be favored by companies and shoppers because it will be more convenient than today's national currencies, which by then will seem quaint because of much disruption to economic life in the last part of the twentieth century."

The above prediction appeared on a 1988 cover story of the *Economist* magazine titled "Get ready for a world currency."[1] At the time, ten years before the introduction of the euro, it sounded incredibly untenable. Today, more than three decades after publication, it still does. In our increasingly fractured world, the idea of a world currency like the phoenix is as elusive as the vision of the Esperanto language. And yet, while the road to a global currency seems unrealistic, the world is taking baby steps toward an evolutionary change in monetary affairs that might, one day and under certain circumstances, give rise to just that.

How will people transact thirty years from now? Will they continue to use colored pieces of paper as means of exchange as they mostly do today or will they virtualize money as they have done in almost every aspect of human life? And if the latter, will the money remain the property of the state or will it be controlled by a non-state virtual community? Could Jeff Bezos issue an Amazon currency? After all, he owns the world's biggest store. Could Mark Zuckerberg issue a Facebook currency? After all, more than 2 billion people have daily relations with his platform. How can we secure money that is not made or backed by anything of value but is merely a combinations of bits, which hackers based in foreign countries can steal? And perhaps the biggest question of all: How can debt dependent governments continue to raise debt if more and more money is diverted to non-sovereign currency? All these questions could not even be asked thirty years ago. If we are to try to answer these questions, we must first take stock of how our money got to where it is today.

**From barter to Bitcoin**

The history of money can be divided into four chapters. It started with millennia of a straightforward **barter system** in which goods were exchanged among people based on their value. With the invention of the wheel, the domestication of horses and the creation of carts, humans were able to expand the geographical scope of their commercial activity and barter was abandoned in favor of **commodity money**, meaning currencies made from precious metals like gold or silver. There was no reason to carry a ton of timber to pay for a barrel of olive oil. A few silver coins facilitated the exchange. But as the world economy continued to expand, carrying heavy chests full of shiny pieces of metal became too cumbersome and increasingly unsafe for the Chinese, Mongol and European merchants who traversed the dangerous steppes of Eurasia at the time. Hence, in 1260, during the Chinese Yuan dynasty, the first paper currency to be used as the predominant medium of exchange in China was issued. Thus was born what is known today as **representative money**, which is paper money backed by physical commodities (think Gold Standard). For the next seven centuries, governments could issue money in proportion to the volume of gold stored in their secure vaults. Paper was just an IOU that could always be redeemed for gold. Merchants no longer had to fear that their ships, loaded with gold, would sink to the bottom of the ocean and their gold would be lost. But the rapid expansion in world population and the explosive economic growth enabled by the Industrial Revolution ushered a new chapter in the 20$^{th}$ century, the messiest of all, that of **fiat money**, money whose value is essentially derived from our collective faith in the governments behind them.

Because most of us are programmed to see governments as stable guarantors of the fiat system, we barely doubt their ability to back up their currency. Odd as it may sound, the system has worked quite well, partly because at least until 1971 the fiat money system was still backed by gold. To be sure, from time to time, a national currency faltered, like in the 2002 crisis of the Argentine peso, but then the international community, spearheaded by the IMF, jumped into action and intervened to save the day so the fiat party could go on. But with the collapse of the Gold Standard and the mounting accumulation of debt, the fiat system has become unsustainable. The reality is that governments always spend beyond their means, people always want to pay less in taxes and receive more benefits, and politicians always try to go along to get along. Over the long run, this toxic combination creates a mountain of debt which eventually leads to insolvency.

To make things worse, the fiat system is based on the principle of fractional reserve banking (FRB) in which banks keep only a fraction of the deposits they receive in cash, freeing up most capital to be loaned out to other parties (which in some ways is good because it creates economic dynamism as more people can start businesses, buy homes, etc.) Under such a system, the money supply is growing exponentially. Credit is the oxygen that allows the cells of our global economy to multiply, but the risk in such rapid growth of the supply of money is that it creates a hall of mirrors effect in which the value of derivatives far exceeds that of real money and tangible assets. To understand the degree of the disconnect, consider that the total value of all of the world's coins, notes, gold, money market accounts as well as saving, checking and time deposit accounts is under $100 trillion. The total value of another tangible asset class, the world's real estate (commercial, residential and agricultural land), is roughly $217 trillion. The total value of all of the world's stocks in 2017 was roughly $73 trillion (This figure obviously fluctuates daily based on the mood of stock markets). They too can be considered tangible assets as they represent companies with real assets. But as we enter the planet of derivatives like futures contracts, swaps, warrants, options and other tools of financial wizardry, the line separating the real and the metaphysical becomes blurred. It is believed that the value of all derivatives is more than the cumulative value of all the asset classes combined. No wonder that in 2008 when the bubble of shady financial instruments like "mortgage-backed securities" and "credit default swaps" burst, the world economy nearly collapsed.

Hiccups and heart attacks aside, overall, the fiat money system has worked remarkably well, leading to unprecedented global prosperity. But it has also resulted in a situation in which two decades into the 21$^{st}$ century the world's debt pile is hovering near a record $244 trillion, which is more than three times the size of the global economy.[2] At some point, the burden of this debt will fall on someone's shoulders. Typically, major historical transformations occur due to the accumulation of such debt levels. We may be in the midst of such a period. In addition to the geopolitical and geoeconomic drivers we have already alluded to in previous chapters, social changes like political gridlock, lack of social cohesion, growing resentment about income inequality, intergenerational tension, general amnesia about the defects of socialism, government overregulation of the financial system, chronic lack of access to credit, the rise of surveillance states, and automation all feed the gathering storm. But when it comes to the creation of a new era of money, the secret spice is technology. The emergence of game changing technologies like distributed ledgers, 5G communication, big data analytics, internet of things, quantum computing and artificial intelligence will change every aspect of human life. They are also poised to facilitate the emergence of digital money.

**Crypto paradox**

Satoshi Nakamoto is probably the most mysterious person in the world. We do not even know if this is a man or a woman, one person or a group of individuals. Perhaps the name is a pseudonym. Indeed, a 21$^{st}$ century John Galt. Yet, Nakamoto is also one of the most influential people of our time—the person behind Bitcoin and the first Blockchain database as well as other important ideas related to the decentralization of the internet. The terms cryptocurrencies, Blockchain and Bitcoin are so widely used today that we are almost tempted to assume that they need no introduction. Also, we are writing this book at a time that the world is down on cryptocurrencies. Bitcoin, which concentrates half of the money put into cryptocurrencies, has demonstrated incredible volatility. It plummeted in 2018 from $19,000 to less than $4,000 only to bounce back above $10,000 several months later. And the total market capitalization of all 2,100 cryptos in circulation went down from three quarters of a trillion dollars in January 2018 to $120 billion a year later. So strong was the disillusionment and popular backlash against cryptos that in October 2018 global economist Nouriel Roubini told the U.S. Senate Committee on Banking, Housing and Community Affairs at a hearing that "crypto is the mother or father of all scams and bubbles" and "Blockchain is the most over-hyped — and least useful — technology in human history."[3]

We see things a bit differently. The 2018 crypto crash should not be viewed as the end of the cryptocurrencies story. To be sure, many of the cryptos that entered the market over the past decade have been flawed in terms of security, scalability and architecture. There have been many teething problems in their operations, which have caused investors to lose millions of dollars. There are also design problems that raise questions about the long-term viability of these cryptos. Bitcoin, for example, was created with a money supply limited to 21 million coins. What happens after all the coins are mined? No one really knows. And since Bitcoin is a completely decentralized system with no one in charge, there is nobody to call and ask. We do not know Satoshi Nakamoto's phone number. The fact that cryptos have become the currency of choice of drug dealers, money launderers, terrorists, hackers and other shady elements of our society has not helped their reputation either.

But while the execution of most of the cryptocurrencies has been marred with troubles, it is the principles behind the idea of a virtual currency we should remain focused on as they are setting the foundation for future monetary architecture. Nixing cryptocurrencies based on their initial performance would be as self-defeating as terminating the mission to put a man on the moon just because Apollo 1 caught fire on the launch pad. If not for Apollo 1, there would have been no Apollo 11. Distributed ledgers, digital currencies and some of the other building blocks of what is likely to be a revolution in monetary affairs could be as consequential to the future of humanity, not the least to the future of the United States, as Neil Armstrong and Buzz Aldrin's moon landing. They are central to the argument of this book so we will spend some time on the basics.

Bitcoin was created in 2009 by a group of people who philosophically have very little faith in the government and who are especially opposed to government manipulation and interference in the financial system. Deeply affected by the crackdown on personal privacy in the aftermath of September 11, enraged by the government's failure to prevent the financial collapse of 2008 and inspired by Satoshi Nakamoto's ideas, they created a peer-to-peer technology, which enables essential functions of currency exchange such as currency issuance, transaction processing and verification to be carried out collectively by a network of anonymous players through the use of encryption techniques that give each digital coin a unique identity which cannot be forged or replicated. The real breakthrough behind Bitcoin was the solution to the nagging problem of double-spending. In a trustless system in which anonymous people transact with each other all over the world, how can we be sure that the same token is not spent more than once? The answer is a distributed ledger called Blockchain where all transactions are recorded simultaneously and the data is shared across a network of multiple sites, geographies and institutions. The self-regulated and totally decentralized ledger is replicated and distributed among thousands of computers called nodes. The Bitcoin ledger, for example, is distributed in more than 10,000 nodes spread over 100 countries. Not controlled by any central authority, every user can police the system, and decisions are made by user consensus. Blockchain is the most popular distributed ledger for cryptocurrencies, though not the only one. Many believe it is not even the best one. The term comes from the ability of its algorithm to aggregate transactions in "blocks" and then add then to a "chain" of existing blocks using a cryptographic signature.

Bitcoins are created digitally through a "mining" process that requires powerful and energy hungry computers to solve complex mathematical problems. Because the coin itself has no central authority behind it, nor is backed by a scarce resource like gold, the mathematical problems are the way to control the expansion of the money supply. The miners compete against each other in a race to solve the puzzles. The winner is awarded with the right to validate a set of Bitcoin transactions comprising a block in what is called "proof-of-work." This wins him 25 coins. Just like each banknote can be distinguished from another by serial numbers and other security features, each Bitcoin has its own unique digital identity. While the first generation of cryptocurrencies captured the imagination of millions around the world, giving rise to an entire ecosystem of investors, developers of digital wallets and operators of Bitcoin exchanges, it is now increasingly apparent that cryptocurrencies cannot live up to the dream of their creators and scale up to become national currencies, not the least global-scale currencies. The chance of any of the first generation cryptocurrencies ever becoming a reserve currency is virtually zero.

There are many reasons for this. One problem is network scalability or what is called Blockchain bloat. In essence, every time transactions are added to the ledger, the Blockchain becomes larger, requiring more memory and processing power. As long as the volume of transactions is moderate, the problem is manageable, but if the number of users and transactions is to grow to the scale of a national currency with millions of users and trillions of transactions, the Bitcoin ledger would run into size limitations. Processing speed is another problem. Today, the number of transactions per second (TPS) the Bitcoin system can process is seven. Visa, in comparison, can handle 1,700 TPS (according to some estimates the theoretical capacity is closer to 24,000 TPS). And even this is nothing in comparison to China's e-commerce platforms. In the first 15 minutes of the 2017 Chinese Singles' Day, the Alibaba e-commerce platform processed 325,000 TPS. If those transactions were to be made in Bitcoins, the system would crash in less than one minute.

Another issue is security. The decentralized nature of cryptocurrencies solves many security problems but it also poses new ones. For example, the 'wallets' that hold the currency have proven vulnerable to theft. In 2018 alone, $1.7 billion worth of cryptos disappeared due to theft and scams. Even the ledger itself could be vulnerable if over 50 percent of the computer processing power for the ledger fell into the hands of a single malevolent individual or organization. These so called "51 percent attacks" have occurred several times. Since the identity of the node owners is unknown and since governments are more likely to have the resources and computing power required to take over the system, it is not out of the realm of possibility that an entire ledger with all of the sensitive information it contains could fall in the hands of a foreign government without our knowledge. Security is also likely to weaken over time as the reward per block continues to decline. The less rewarding mining becomes, the weaker the incentive of the miners to keep the system secure. One way to address the security problems associated with user anonymity is to shift from the current Bitcoin Blockchain to something called permissioned Blockchain which operates without the proof-of-work and where validation of transactions is not made by any anonymous member of the network but rather through highly trusted administrators who serve as gatekeepers and allow new users to enter the club.

While in theory there are solutions to all of these problems, in most cases if the crypto network were to implement them, the solutions would create even bigger problems. Vitalik Buterin, founder of one of Bitcoin's chief competitors, Ethereum, coined the term "Scalability Trilemma." Just like in the case of the engineers' triangle—Fast, good or cheap, pick any two—the Scalability Trilemma of DLT developers is how to optimize the three prerequisites of a crypto system: scalability, security and decentralization. The choice of any two will come at the expense of the third. For example, to achieve scalability, the number of nodes could be reduced, but this means the system would become more centralized. And even if all the technical problems were miraculously solved, there would still be two major constraints to mass adoption of currencies. First is the reluctance of most businesses to accept them as a form of payment. Cryptocurrencies are disconnected from the existing payments infrastructure and this makes it challenging for their users to realize them. Second, there is always the risk that governments might outlaw the conversion of cryptocurrencies into cash, preventing their users from realizing their wealth, or even worse, might ban them altogether. Governments have been slow to react to the rise of cryptocurrencies, and, by and large, they have taken their time in passing judgment about them. This is partly because cryptos are technologically complex but mostly because for the time being they are too small to pose a real threat to governments' authority. Being a tiny asset class, they are treated as a gimmick. This could quickly change if and when they gain mass adoption and begin to challenge traditional currencies. In other words, cryptos can be tolerated as long as their market cap is in the billions of dollars—but not in the trillions.

What is more likely to happen is that after a period of inquiry and hesitation, governments will ultimately open up to the opportunities and advantages offered by virtual currencies. Building on the experiences and the innovation behind Bitcoin and its cousins, they will introduce central bank digital currencies (CBDC) that are more fitted to the open and transparent nature of a national and international financial system. A CBDC is a virtual currency that is issued by the state and has a legal tender status. In other words, just like fiat currencies, it is backed by the government and it is part of the country's money supply. For the crypto community, the idea of a CBDC which allows governments to track every slice of pizza we buy is horrifying. This is not what they put their sweat into. But like it or not, the trajectory is clear. Starved for cash and enamored with the idea of achieving full control over our movements and purchases, it is just a matter of time before governments will realize that CBDC is exactly what they need. The reason is that in the end, as Erik Townsend compellingly argued in his book *Beyond Blockchain: The Death of the Dollar and the Rise of Digital Currency*, nobody stands to gain more from digital currencies than government.

"Digital currency systems could easily be engineered with the exact opposite of Bitcoin, embracing a design which enables government to monitor, regulate, and control every single payment that occurs anywhere on earth," he wrote.[4] Considering the ideological underpinning of Satoshi Nakamoto and his ilk, this turn of events could go down in history as the "crypto paradox."

For now, no CBDC exists. On the other hand, it is difficult to find a central bank that is not looking into the idea. China, the U.S., Australia, Hong Kong, Singapore, Norway, South Korea, Switzerland, Spain, Uruguay, Malta and the UK are just some of the countries that have commissioned feasibility studies and conducted simulations to examine the pros and cons of this concept. The Swedish central bank is perhaps the most far along in its progress toward launching the e-Krona. So far, however, most central bankers—a conservative bunch—are unenthusiastic. They are concerned that CBDC could constrain the ability of commercial banks to retain retail customers and even more so they fear that a digital currency could accelerate the speed and scale of a run on a bank during periods of market volatility. This will make commercial banks more dependent on the central bank. However, central bankers also see the advantages of CBDC. Digital money, for example, improves the efficiency of financial transactions, as there is no need for intermediaries and bank fees. Money can be easily transferred from payer to payee. It also increases people's participation in the banking system. It enhances transparency, improves tax collection and can streamline the distribution of social benefits. Besides, many societies are moving away from physical money anyway. A growing number of countries have been limiting the use of cash with the stated goal of fighting money laundering and tax evasion. This trend will continue as humanity entrenches itself deeper and deeper in the digital economy. This is why it is likely that central bank skepticism will eventually be replaced with enthusiasm.

While government bureaucrats ponder the pros and cons of digital currencies, on June 18th, 2019, a shot across the bow was fired from Facebook's headquarters in Menlo Park, California with the announcement of the launch of Libra, the company's digital Blockchain-based currency, and a payment platform called Calibra which would enable cross-border money transfers. This ambitious project, while falling short of being a CBDC, reminds us all that the revolution in monetary affairs may not necessarily originate from the quarters of any single government or central bank but rather from the private sector.

## Facebuck?

The digital revolution has already changed society in numerous ways, proving time and again that no legacy powerbase is immune to competition from a digital platform. The mainstream media learned the hard way about the power of the blogosphere and the twitterverse; retail chains have been effectively taken over by e-commerce platforms; accountants, taxi drivers and travel agents are being displaced by more efficient digital platforms like TurboTax, Uber and Expedia. Even intelligence and law enforcement agencies often find themselves outmaneuvered by armies of Davids like WikiLeaks and smart and dedicated netizens. Thanks to high barriers to entry and a tough regulatory environment, with the exception of some peer-to-peer payment platforms, to date the banking sector has been almost unchallenged by the digital economy players. This changed once previously hip startups like Facebook, Amazon and Google turned into insatiable Pac-Man-like monsters who swallow every competitor in their path. Apparently, these companies cannot resist the temptation to enter the incredibly lucrative financial sector. Facebook, which has daily relations with a quarter of humanity (if it had existed in the Fifties, the Stasi wouldn't have had to work so hard) and which has already changed social interaction in more than one way, was the first to enter the race to reshape the global financial system. It announced a currency, Libra, and the Calibra wallet supporting it, which will enable users to move money around the globe with a very small commission, perhaps even free of charge, via apps owned by Facebook like WhatsApp and Facebook Messenger as well as dedicated ones designed for Android and iOS users. For Facebook, this is not only a good way to make money but also an opportunity to expand its social network into the developing world where hundreds of millions of users lack access to financial services and credit. According to the World Bank, global remittances reached $689 billion in 2018.[5] Existing payment services like Paypal, Western Union and MoneyGram charge hefty commissions of roughly 7 percent, ripping off the poorest people in the world. With Libra, money could move instantaneously and cheaply, providing access to financial services to the 1.7 billion people who today don't even own a bank account. Unlike Bitcoin and most other cryptos that are backed by thin air, Libra will be backed by a basket of financial assets that are both safe and liquid, including fiat currencies like dollars, euros, Swiss francs and Japanese yens as well as sovereign bonds. These assets will be bought with the revenues Facebook and its partners generate from selling Libras. The profits of the operation will be made from interest arbitrage: Facebook and its partners will not pay interest on users' Libra deposits but they will generate returns on the money that goes into the Libra reserve.

Facebook is launching the Libra at a time it is under scrutiny and criticism for its monopolistic practices and for a string of scandals including privacy violations, spreading fake news and facilitating the alleged Russian meddling in the 2016 elections. A 2019 poll showed that 60 percent of Americans do not trust the company to protect their data.[6] To calm fears about the company's misuse of users' data, Facebook established in Switzerland the Libra Association, a non-government organization controlled by stakeholders like Visa, Paypal, MasterCard, Uber and of course Facebook itself, each contributing a seed investment of $10 million. Facebook vows that the user data associated with Libra transactions will not be shared with the company or its affiliates. We've heard that before. It further promises that it will have no special role in the Libra Association and that no single member of the association's 100-member governing board will have more than 1 percent of the votes. In the U.S. Senate, there are also 100 members but as we know only a few of them really matter. No wonder there are countless uncertainties about the new venture. One of them has to do with the stability of the Libra. In order for the new currency to be a reliable means of exchange and store of value, it must be able to maintain its value over time, a trait that to date no cryptocurrency has been able to demonstrate. In fact, even big and well-established central banks often struggle to confront currency speculators who try to short or long the currency for a quick gain. It's one thing for drug dealers, money launderers and speculators to lose 20 percent in one week on a Bitcoin transaction. It's quite another for a Filipino guest worker in Dubai sending remittances to his poor family at home. Could the Libra succeed in maintain stability where so many central banks, let alone cryptos, have failed? Facebook believes that stability is a function of volume. The company already has a 2.4 billion strong customer base, which could be recruited to use the Libra. WhatsApp alone has 1.5 billion registered users. Facebook Messenger has 1.3 billion. In addition, Facebook has relationships with 7 million advertisers and 90 million small businesses. It also brought on board the Libra Association companies with a large customer base like Spotify, eBay and Lyft who could help popularize the new currency. This gigantic user base positions the Libra in a much better starting point than cryptos like Bitcoin and Ethereum which failed to scale. Facebook believes that a rapid and widespread adoption of the Libra could cushion the new currency from market fluctuations and ensure its stability. So will it being pegged to a basket of stable currencies and low-volatility assets, including bank deposits and government securities.

However, both the potential user base and the link to fiat currencies can be sources of problems. Facebook wants to go to market with reserve assets totaling a billion dollars. But what if the Libra's launch proved to be a great success and within weeks demand for Libras were to reach tens or hundreds of billions of dollars? Will Facebook be ready to meet the demand and acquire enough assets to back up its currency? And what about the so-called Blockchain bloat which prevents the system from scaling fast enough to serve thousands of transactions per second without delays and interruptions? To address this, the Libra will be hosted on a permissioned Blockchain, meaning only a few trusted entities can keep track of the ledger. But who will those trusted entities be? Who will determine the identity of the nodes to ensure they are not foreign powers or criminal elements? And how does one secure such a new digital bank from all the hackers who will no doubt find the challenge of bringing it down irresistible? To be sure, linking the Libra to sovereign currencies can shield it from price fluctuations, but it will also give the Libra Association inordinate power no non-state actor has ever had before. Once hundreds of billions of dollars rest in the reserves of the Libra Association, its board will be able to decide on the mix of currencies in its reserve basket, wielding influence over exchange rates among sovereign currencies. The Libra Association could quite easily find itself with more power and influence than the IMF, which currently decides on the composition of its SDR. As a major bond buyer, it would also be able to decide which country's sovereign bonds should be purchased and which not. Mark Zuckerberg will be able to decide if debt distressed countries like Italy and Greece go under or stay afloat. By what authority? Will the EU be comfortable fining Facebook for privacy violations, as it has in the past, with that knowledge in mind? Such decisions are political and could have major implications for national economies, trade relations among countries and the overall geopolitical environment. Such power in the hands of a bunch of American executives operating out of a Swiss jurisdiction and led by a socially awkward CEO like Zuckerberg is not likely to sit well with most governments which have yet to approve the Libra as legal tender. Facebook deplatforms users whose views it deems unacceptable; only a fool would believe it will not use its financial platform in a similar manner as a political carrot and stick. The Libra Association will have to comply with political pressures by any government under the jurisdiction of which it operates or else.

If Libra does catch on, it could pose a challenge to central banks' authority as well as to global currency trends. To begin with, it will reduce the demand for currencies like the dollar. The more people who use the Libra for online transactions, the less use there will be for those currencies, and central banks will need to print less of them. This could limit their ability to stabilize their economies. Commercial banks will also suffer because less money will be funneled through them. Hundreds of billions worth of bonds are currently being bought for a fee by millions of customers via commercial banks. In the era of Libra, these commercial papers will be bought directly by one gigantic wholesale buyer—the Libra Association—draining banks' profits at a time global banking is already facing serious problems.

U.S. regulators have already begun to grapple with some of the dilemmas presented by Zuckerberg and his team. The House Financial Services Committee and the Senate Banking Committee held hearings about the Libra, urging Facebook to halt its project until Congress studies the implications for the global financial system. Legislation barring giant digital companies from entering the financial services sector, if passed, could crush Facebook's audacious bid to create a global digital currency. This will be an unfolding drama which will put to test governments' willingness to share power with gigantic, profit driven, corporations and it will take years before the battle for financial hegemony is decided. But regardless of the outcome, the Libra may have already changed the global monetary architecture: it has instilled a sense of urgency in China to do exactly what Facebook has attempted, setting off a chain reaction which can no longer be reversed.

Facebook and the rest of the FAANG companies are viewed in China as a secret arm of the U.S. government. Companies like Google and Facebook and their subsidiaries like YouTube, Instagram, Twitter and WhatsApp have been blocked in the country for years mainly for what the CPC views as their subversive potential. The Chinese closely observe the coziness between FAANG and the so-called Deep State. Just like many Americans believe that Huawei is linked to the Chinese state apparatus, Chinese too are convinced that Silicon Valley is the fiefdom of the U.S. intelligence community. Amazon's $600 million deal to provide cloud computing services to the CIA and Edward Snowden's revelations about the U.S. government's forbidden relations with America's technology companies have only reinforced this view.

"The key to Facebook's economic success," in the words of Scott Galloway, "is a cocktail of vision, agile execution, sociopathy, and a market that had stuck its chin so far out it slipped a disk — the media industry."[7] But in the eyes of the Chinese there is an even more important key to the company's success—the U.S. government. Nothing could be more anathematic to the Chinese government and corporate culture than the company's motto "move fast and break things," and it would be inconceivable for a Chinese corporate leader to claim, as did Zuckerberg, that his company "is more like a government than a company." From the Chinese perspective, there is no chance that Washington would allow a company to - just like that - mine the brains of over 2 billion people, map their relationship networks and track their every move; an undertaking like Facebook, let alone the Libra project, could have never emerged absent some secret pact between the "Deep State" and Menlo Park. This view is reinforced by the fact that all of the members of the Libra Association are American corporations.

In the midst of an escalating economic war between China and the United States, suspicion and nervousness run high. "We will keep a close eye on the new global digital currency," said Wang Xin, director of the People Bank of China (PBoC) Research Bureau few days after the announcement of Libra.[8] Beijing views the Libra not as competition to the dollar but as its proxy - a tool to undermine China's effort to internationalize the yuan and threaten the country's cross-border payments, monetary policy and financial sovereignty. As mentioned before, the plan for Libra is to be pegged to a basket of currencies, but the yuan is not one of them. It took China a great deal of effort to include its currency in the IMF's SDR basket. Exclusion of the yuan from the Libra reserve would be a setback. In the mind of Chinese officials, the Libra will enable the U.S. government to operate two parallel currencies: the real dollar and a surrogate dollar. Each could be manipulated at will to advance Washington's financial goals. Furthermore, the Libra's penetration into the developing world, particularly in the Belt and Road territories, would run against China's efforts to enhance yuan exposure and increase local currency use in that part of the world. Facebook's pledge to stay away from user data will not be bought in Beijing (nor, given Facebook's track record, should it be bought anywhere else.) In the eyes of the CPC, the Libra is merely a new addition to America's Surveillance Intelligence Complex and another tool to extend U.S. financial jurisdiction. It should be resisted at all costs, and the only way of doing so is to be there first with a cross-border digital currency, one with Chinese characteristics.

## Blockchina

To date, China has expressed mixed feelings about virtual currencies. On the one hand, it more or less rejected cryptos which it views—no surprise here—as a threat to its centralized financial system. In 2017, the government banned cryptocurrency exchanges and initial coin offerings (ICOs). On the other hand, it is very interested in the Blockchain space, particularly in permissioned Blockchains, which offer more control over users' identity. The Chinese State Council embraced Blockchain in its 13th Five-Year Plan; it accelerated investment in DLT and enhanced the research in digital currencies beyond any other country. The PBoC is leading the charge through its Digital Currency Research Institute (DCRI), which filed more digital currency patents than any other entity in China in 2017. The PBoC has been hiring engineers and legal experts; it established fintech centers in Shenzhen and Nanjing, launched a Blockchain trading finance platform in Shenzhen and established a pilot zone in Hainan Province.[9] China may not be interested in cryptocurrencies like Bitcoin, but it is extremely interested in Libra-style stablecoins that can be pegged to currency, or to traded commodities such as precious metals. In 2018, the official publication of the PBoC ran a piece on yuan-pegged stablecoins, arguing that China should double down on its efforts to support domestic institutions to issue yuan-pegged crypto stablecoins.[10] If China's gold reserves are indeed much more substantial than its official numbers state, this would provide China with the ability to offer the first ever central bank digital stablecoin with a gold-convertibility standard and possibly a complementary digital bond market. This would give its CBDC unique qualities that cannot be found in most fiat currencies, hence increasing the appeal for central bankers to make it part of their reserve assets.

In some ways, China is an ideal laboratory for the introduction of CBDC. First, it is already a de facto cashless society. The largest banknote in circulation is 100 yuan (about $15), making big cash transactions cumbersome. While cash is not practical, credit cards have never become mainstream in the country. This is why China has become the leading society in mobile payments. So much so that almost half of the world's digital payments in 2017 were made in China.[11] Almost every person and business in China has a unique WeChat and Alipay QR code by which they can transact. So rare has cash become that foreign visitors with no local bank account find it increasingly difficult to get around. Second, China's digital giants are highly centralized and, while not state owned, are aligned with the regime. China's largest internet company Tencent is the mother company of WeChat, whose daily users surpassed one billion in 2019, and QQ and instant messaging and web portal also with a billion active users. Tencent is also a partial owner of JD.com, China's leading e-commerce platform second only to Alibaba Group. If China were to offer an alternative to the Libra, Tencent would be best positioned to lead the charge. Third, the Chinese government is deeply engaged in big-data-meets-big-brother wholesale data collection, monitoring and profiling of its citizens as part of its plan to integrate financial credit scoring systems with measures of social behavior. The combination of a cashless society and a social credit system combined with the impetus of not being second to a U.S.-led digital currency like the Libra, provide fertile ground for the introduction of a Chinese CBDC. This is all made particularly easier by the fact that the Chinese banking system which provides the backbone and clearing for digital transactions is essentially an instrument of the Chinese state, while BATH-JD, China's tech giants—Baidu, Alibaba, Tencent, Huawei, JD.com and Didi, the equivalent of

America's FAANG—which collect, store and process the data, are all aligned with the government, though it is hard to determine how much influence the CPC really has over their daily operations.

It is premature to tell what a Chinese digital currency might look like, if and when it will be launched, how it will be governed and how it will be received by other countries. China decides slowly but when it finally moves, it moves fast. This is something to keep in mind as the United States tries to ensure that it does not find itself, like in the case of 5G, lagging behind its competitors. One of Facebook's talking points is that if it is not permitted to launch someone else will. This should not be a reason for Congress and the U.S. government to hand over the keys to our financial future to Facebook or any other company for that matter. It should rather be a call for action to the government to catch up with the irreversible trend of the digitization of the monetary system and work toward a private-public partnership, creating a dollar-based digital currency that offers all the social benefits of Libra, especially in empowering the world's poor, but without the pitfalls associated with private sector reflexes. Backed by America's vast gold reserves and/or by its trillions of dollars' worth of Treasury bonds and supported by America's rule of law and financial best practices, such a currency would be more appealing to the world. This is no small project, and it should grow from an understanding that the rest of the world is no longer satisfied with the status quo. The problem is that to a large extent Americans are. Bullish about their economic hegemony, Americans are inattentive to the perfect storm that is gathering over the horizon. This is imprudent not only because America's competitors are now super-motivated to transform the monetary playing field, but also because as we describe in the next chapter there has never been a bigger disconnect between the way Americans view the strength of their economy and its true health.

# 7  ALICE IN WONDERLAND ECONOMICS

> How did you go bankrupt? Two ways.
> Gradually, then suddenly.
> *Ernest Hemingway, The Sun Also Rises*

The collective desire of the dollar insurgents to append the global financial order is indeed strong and growingly impactful. But it is doubtful that their effort to erode the dollar's international primacy will gain much traction as long as U.S. growth, prestige and alliances remain strong. It is America's actions - rather than its adversaries' - that will determine its prospects for global leadership for the rest of the 21$^{st}$ century. Indeed, the future of the dollar is much more dependent on the decisions made at the White House, Capitol Hill and, most important, the Marriner S. Eccles Building, the home of the Federal Reserve Board in Washington, than on those made in Beijing, Brussels or Moscow, let alone Tehran and Caracas. A decade after the global financial crisis, the United States is at a critical juncture, and the monetary policies that will be adopted in the coming years by the Fed, the current and next administrations and the U.S. Congress will probably be the most consequential in the history of the Republic. This is not an overstatement. The future of the dollar as the world's reserve currency is probably the number one security issue we have as a nation—far more important than much touted threats like North Korea, ISIS or Russia and even China. Let us be clear: it is the single most important factor determining America's superpower status. Yet it is not even a footnote in our political discourse. The mainstream media, even the financial media, have a blind spot on the matter. Secure in the complacent inertia of our hegemonic mindset, we ignore the red lights flickering on our economic dashboard. To determine how precarious our intermediate and long-term financial well-being is and what is at stake, we should first understand how all the gears that move our economy—the dollar, interest rates, our national debt, etc.—interlock and how failure to harmonize them could jeopardize our future.

## Debt withdrawal syndrome

Modern day governments tend to spend beyond their means and must therefore borrow money from their own people and from other governments to meet their budgetary obligations. In 2017, only 41 countries in the world experienced budget surpluses. Most of the world is in debt. As mentioned before, in 2019 global debt reached an all-time high of $244 trillion - almost three times global GDP.[1] The United States comprises less than five percent of the world's population yet its federal government accounts for more than one tenth of the world's debt, a whopping $22 trillion. U.S. per capita federal debt has doubled since 2008, hitting $67,000 in 2019. The federal debt per taxpayer has surpassed $180,000. This figure is in fact much higher if one adds to the federal debt household, business, state and local governments' debts as well as the debts and obligations owned by financial institutions. Adding these inflates our collective debt to an eye-popping $73 trillion—about the size of the world's GDP.[2] Yet, due to the strong economy and superpower status that the United States has managed to sustain, borrowing from foreign countries and domestic lenders has been more or less a walk in the park. For all its problems, the country is still viewed as stable, rich and dependable, and therefore most central bankers have no qualms about buying American bonds. In fact, the more chaotic and uncertain the world becomes, especially in light of the weakness of the Eurozone and the slowing Chinese economy, the more countries are drawn to the safe haven of U.S. Treasuries. That said, being the world's largest debtor nation presents major problems, and as time goes by these problems become increasingly consequential.

Borrowing money means that at some point the money must be repaid to the lender with pre-agreed interest. The loan itself can be rolled over for decades—it took Britain 100 years to pay back its loans from World War I—but the interest must always be paid on time. As long as the overall debt burden is low, the cost of debt servicing is manageable. But beyond a certain level of debt, interest payments become so large that they crowd out other government expenditures like defense, health, infrastructure, education and foreign aid. In 2008, U.S. federal debt stood at around $8 trillion, total government revenue was $2.52 trillion and the interest on the debt was $187 billion. Ten years later, with the debt at $22 trillion and government revenue hitting $3.33 trillion, the interest for fiscal year 2018 was $325 billion. In other words, both the debt and the interest on it grew much more than the revenues. Things could have been much worse if not for the fact for the duration of the decade interest rates were held at near zero. As we will explain later, rates will eventually crawl up and this means a heavier interest burden. According to the Congressional Budget Office, within a decade, as more bonds reach their date of maturity, the cost of interest payments will surpass $900 billion. For some perspective, our national defense budget for 2020 is $738 billion.[3] This means that future generations will likely pay for our habitual overspending as they are called to foot our collective bill. To twist the biblical adage: the fathers eat sweet grapes, and the children cannot afford the dental treatment.

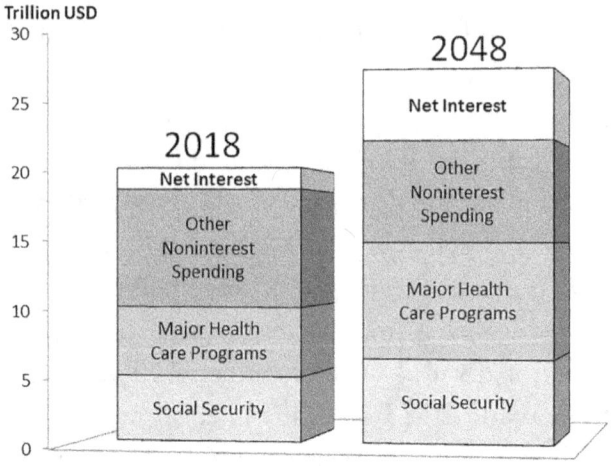

Interest on the national debt will surpass social security and defense spending based on CBO's extended baseline. Source: CBO

The government must service its debt religiously or else it risks having its credit rating downgraded, which means that lenders would demand higher bond yields to justify the risk, and the cost of borrowing would rise. In 2011, after Congress yet again voted to raise the debt ceiling, for the first time U.S. federal government rating was downgraded by Standard & Poor's (S&P), one of the leading credit rating agencies, triggering a market selloff. The 2019 government shutdown again raised fears of a downgrade. Downgrades are a nightmare scenario for the U.S. government as they can immediately translate into higher bond yields and therefore higher debt servicing costs. This is the last thing the government wants. If it is up to Washington, interest rates should remain as low as possible for as long as possible. Low interest rates not only lower the cost of debt servicing but they also mean that cheap money can flow into the economy through lending, thus stimulating consumer spending and entrepreneurship. Increased economic activity would in turn produce higher tax revenues, which is good. But persistent low interest rates can also cause painful economic dislocations: they can cause capital outflows to higher-interest countries; they depress saving, forcing people to divert their money to stocks and real estate, inflating dangerous bubbles in these sectors, and they fuel an entire web of interlocking obligations, many of them shady, known as derivatives. A derivative is in essence a contract between two or more parties that is tied to an underlying financial asset like stocks, bonds, commodities, mortgages, market indices, etc. The problem is that the basic underlying asset is repackaged and sold so many times that a huge gap develops between the inherent value of the asset and the amount of phantom money generated from selling it over and over again. One simple way to understand derivatives is to imagine a chair in the middle of an empty room whose walls and ceiling are covered with mirrors. A person walking into the room sees hundreds of chairs reflected from one mirror onto another. But in reality there is only one chair in the room. All the others are worthless reflections. And the more mirrors are added to the walls, the more chair reflections can be counted. This is why derivatives are so difficult to quantify. According to the Bank of International Settlements, the total global over-the-counter derivatives is roughly $600 trillion—more than the global debt, global real estate and all of the world's stock markets, gold and cash combined.[4] With so much phantom money already in the system and with low interest rates providing incentives to hang more and more mirrors on the walls, in other words create more and more derivatives, the global economy is standing on a very shaky foundation.

Just imagine what happens when interest rates climb and all those trillions that inflated the derivatives bubble begin to migrate to greener pastures. No wonder Warren Buffet called derivatives in

2002 "financial weapons of mass destruction."[5] But perhaps the most troubling aspect of perpetually low interest rates is that they deny central banks, especially the Fed, the monetary tools they need to defend the economy when the next financial crisis hits. Interest rates are like fire extinguishers. When the economy is in trouble, central banks can lower rates in order to stimulate borrowing and investment and through this generate economic activity. But when rates are so low that there is not much room to go down further, the next crisis could look like a house on fire with empty fire extinguishers. Because other major economies have followed the United States in keeping their rates at near zero, their fire extinguishers are also empty. This means that when the fire starts—and at one point or another it will—it could easily consume not only the American house but the entire neighborhood.

The Fed controls not only interest rates but also the money supply that it regulates through open market operations (OMO), which is buying and selling government bonds in the open market. Due to a slower than expected recovery from the global financial crisis, the Fed used an unconventional measure called quantitative easing (QE) - buying trillions of dollars of government bonds in order to flood the market with cheap money. This way, from 2008 until 2014, the Fed bumped up its balance sheet from $1 trillion to $4.5 trillion. The problem is that financial markets have become so addicted to cheap money that they throw a hissy fit every time the Fed shows signs that it is about to take steps to drain liquidity and raise interest rates, and this puts pressure on the Fed, not to mention the administration and the sleepy watchdog called Congress, to leave rates at their low level. Nobody knows how this game of chicken between the Fed and the market will end, but for the time being the Fed seems to be the one blinking first. After raising interest rates four times in 2018, the Fed surprised markets in early 2019 by calling a time-out in raising rates, which may last until 2021. In fact, in July 2019 -- under heavy pressure from President Trump who tweeted on July 6, "Our most difficult problem is not our competitors, it is the Federal Reserve!" -- it decided to cut rates despite the strong economy. If it were up to the administration, the Fed would always acquiescence and interest rates would remain forever low. In April 2019, President Trump's Director of the National Economic Council Larry Kudlow predicted that the Fed would not raise interest rates "in my lifetime."[6] He was only 72 at the time.

In the annals of modern economic history, there is no reference case for the long-term consequences of so many years of near zero interest rates. We are in uncharted territory at a point in which financial markets are so distorted by artificial cash injections that any reasonable person must take into account that a day of reckoning may be looming on the horizon. Sadly, the U.S. government does not see it this way. Its assumption as demonstrated in a 2019 Treasury Department presentation is that the interest rate on a 10-year Treasury note would go up by less than 1 percent over the next ten years and that rates will remain flat between 2022 and 2028.[7] But over the next ten years, the government is projected to borrow an additional $12 trillion, and if anyone believes an amount of money roughly equivalent to the GDP of China can be raised at such low rates when the global economy is slowing down, trust in the American economy is eroding and China and Russia are leading an anti-dollar jihad, we have a bridge to sell him as well.

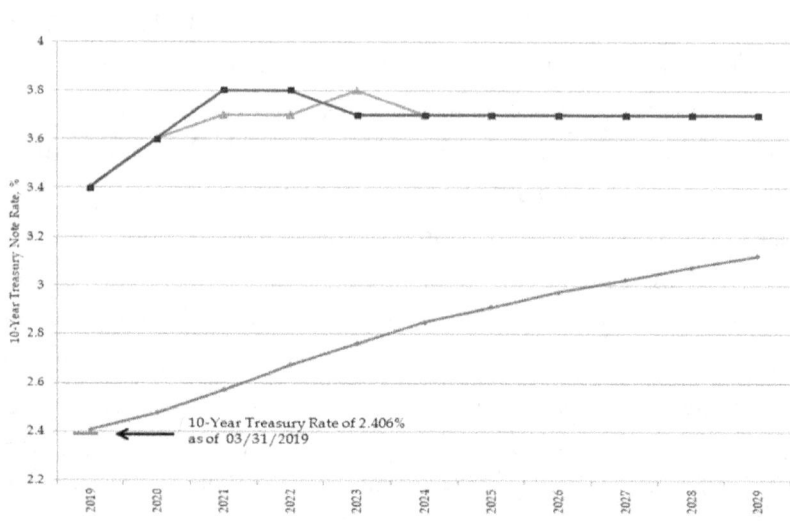

In the eyes of the US government interest rates
will remain flat indefinitely
Source: US Department of Treasury

## How America learned to stop worrying and love the debt bomb

A decade ago in February 2009 when U.S. national debt was half of what it is today, a group of fiscal conservative activists launched the Tea Party movement, named after the Boston Tea Party of 1773, which triggered the American Revolution. Members of the movement, outraged by Obama's Homeowners Affordability and Stability Act, which aimed to provide aid to Americans whose homes were foreclosed as a result of the Great Recession, as well by the deficits about to be created by Obama's Affordable Care Act, called for reduction of the national debt and the federal deficit through a cut in government spending. The group rallied all over the country and endorsed numerous candidates in House and Senate races. In the 2010 mid-term elections, Tea Party candidates won five of ten contested Senate races and 40 of 130 contested House races. Overall, the movement had a huge influence on the Republican Party, but not for long. By 2012, the Tea Party was already on a downward trajectory and its influence in the GOP was waning. Its co-founder Congresswoman Michele Bachmann, who even ran for president in 2012 carrying the banner of fiscal conservatism, retired from politics in 2015. In today's Washington, fiscal conservatism is genuinely espoused by a mere handful of politicians. The rest pay lip service to the need to shrink the deficit, but when it comes to voting on raising the debt ceiling, they all say "Aye." The White House, too, has been mute on the issue. Since 2013, the beginning of President Obama's second term in office, the U.S. national debt has grown by 55 percent, yet the need to address the mounting debt was not raised even once in the following six State of the Union Addresses delivered by Presidents Obama and Trump. The latter even called himself "the king of debt."

Even more troubling is the tendency to accept and even glorify red ink through new ideological-economic constructs created by some of America's top economic thinkers.[8] A choir of economic luminaries like legendary investor Warren Buffett, former Chair of the White House Council of Economic Advisers Jason Furman and former Treasury Secretary Lawrence Summers argue that America can afford to be less concerned about budget deficits and debt.[9] "It's time for Washington to put away its debt obsession," the last two argued in a 2018 essay in *Foreign Affairs* magazine titled "Who is Afraid of Budget Deficits."[10] Well, America's dollar denominated debt may no longer be Washington's obsession, but it is becoming Beijing's, Tokyo's, Brussels', London's, Paris' and Delhi's. The world is increasingly unwilling to accept America's exorbitant privilege. Clearly, the U.S. political class is not ready to level with its citizenry and make the tough choices needed to shrink the deficit. Republicans continue to hail the benefits of additional tax cuts while pushing new expenditures from walling the southern border to new military programs like establishing a Space Force and launching a new nuclear arms race with Russia and China. The Democrats' plans are equally divorced from the fiscal reality. A multi-trillion dollar Green New Deal that includes a zero carbon economy, free college, free healthcare and universal income has become a rallying cry for progressive Democrats as they try to retake the White House and the Senate in 2020.

How will we pay for all of this? Deficits don't matter, they say. "We can't afford to let deficit politics stand in the way of an ambitious Green New Deal," wrote the ideologues behind the plan, Andres Bernal, Greg Carlock and Stephanie Kelton, Professor of Public Policy and Economics at Stony Brook University who has become the economic guru of progressives like Bernie Sanders and Alexandria Ocasio-Cortez.[11] When confronted with the unaffordability of their plan, Green New Deal advocates invoke a new and increasingly popular economic school of thought which has become known as Modern Monetary Theory (MMT) also referred to by cynics as the Free Lunch theory of economics. MMT echoes famous economist John Maynard Keynes' permissive approach toward the expansion of budget deficits, except that Keynes' theory was to be applied during periods of high unemployment, while MMT advocates see deficits as an all-weather remedy. The main premise behind the MMT, in the words of Kelton, is that because the U.S. dollar is a public monopoly, "the Federal government can never run out of money, it can never face a solvency problem […] it never has to worry about finding the money in order to be able to spend."[12] Kelton, whose bible on MMT called *The Deficit Myth: Modern Monetary Theory and Creating an Economy for the People* is timed to come out just ahead of the 2020 election, argues that deficits in education, health care, social equality or environmental protection are essentially of the same social and moral status as deficits in money and therefore it is good policy to deepen the money deficit in order to close these social deficits. Hence, because the government borrows in U.S. dollars, which it prints, deficits should not matter as long as they serve to close social gaps and address environmental problems. The government should be allowed to run them in perpetuity simply by printing more dollars.[13]

The new trend of falling in love with deficits and debts feels like a remake of Stanley Kubrick's classic film *Dr. Strangelove or: How I Learned to Stop Worrying and Love the Bomb,* only that in its 2019 version, the bomb is not nuclear but a fiscal one. This is a classic case of cognitive dissonance, a common psychological situation in which one's behavior conflicts with one's belief or values. The conflict is so unsettling that it forces the conflicted person to adopt new beliefs about his or her behavior. Most smokers are fully aware of the harmful impact their habit may have on their health and longevity. To reconcile this knowledge with their conscious decision to continue smoking, they tend to alter their belief, persuading themselves that "in the end it's all in the genes" or constructing an argument that smoking is actually a life saver because it makes them more relaxed and hence protects them from what they believe is a bigger menace: stress or overeating. Similarly, Americans are addicted to debt, but the deep and unsettling sense of impending economic ruin the mounting debt will eventually bring, not to mention the sense of guilt for imposing it on future generations, brings many to rationalize the current path by persuading themselves that debt is actually a good thing, or at the very least something we should not worry about. To the contrary, we should have more and more of it. For debt apologists like Professor Kelton, Japan is a good example why we should pile up more debt. Japan's debt-to-GDP ratio is double that of America's and it is doing just fine, she argues, as if the fact that a chain-smoker—or a Russian roulette player—made it into his 90s makes the habit OK. Smoking eventually kills—and so does debt. If the United States today held the debt level of Japan, its interest payments on this debt would stand at a jaw-dropping sum of more than trillion dollars a year.

## The trade deficit

In her defense of debt, Kelton argued that the U.S. "never has to worry about finding the money in order to be able to spend."[14] This is true. To now there has always been someone around the world willing to underwrite our debt. One reason for this is the trade deficit, meaning that the value of the goods and services the United States imports exceeds the value of the goods and services it exports. In 2019, the U.S. trade deficit was $875 billion, roughly half of it with China. Because bilateral trade is mostly carried out in dollars, the bigger the trade deficit, the bigger the pile of dollars accumulating in the coffers of America's top trading partners: China, Canada, Mexico, Japan, Germany, South Korea and others. These countries could keep their surplus dollars in cash accounts or buy gold, but neither option pays any interest. Their central bankers would much rather buy interest-bearing U.S. Treasuries which, provided the U.S. maintains its creditworthiness, they can easily liquidate as needed. Hence, as long as the United States is viewed as a reliable debtor, its trade deficit essentially generates the fuel that allows the U.S. to issue more debt.

Trade deficits have never been a major source of concern for American policymakers. Due to the special status of the United States as the world's largest economy and the dollar as the world reserve currency, the U.S. could escape some of the problems smaller countries would face had they run similar trade deficits. But all of this changed once Donald Trump entered the White House. Trump's economic doctrine views trade deficits as evidence that certain foreign governments—China, South Korea, Japan, Canada, Mexico and Germany to name a few—are not playing fair in international trade and are taking advantage of the United States. Trump blamed trade deficits for negatively affecting growth and for denying the United States millions of jobs (even though at the time unemployment was at a 50-year low), insisting on new trade deals that would shrink the trade deficit. At the same time, the Trump administration's policies, especially the tax cuts, increased the federal deficit to almost $1 trillion a year. This, coming on the heels of 16 years of Presidents George W. Bush and Barack Obama, who collectively grew U.S. debt by nearly $15 trillion with endless wars, corporate bailouts, tax cuts and entitlement spending. In other words, Trump attempted to do something that is inherently contradictory: increase government spending and reduce the tax burden and at the same time eliminate the very same trade deficits that essentially help the U.S. fill the fiscal hole created by spending much more than it takes in in taxes.

To make matters worse, global growth has become anemic, which means that foreign central banks, which already have high dollar exposure, have less money and even lesser motivation to spend on buying additional U.S. bonds. The implication is clear: with less foreign money available to buy U.S. debt, and with foreign countries frustrated by U.S. behavior, Washington will soon face increasing difficulties in raising money abroad. It will be forced to raise more and more of its money at home. In the short term, U.S. government entities like Social Security and pension funds could increase their holding to cover for diminishing demand abroad. In other words, the government will be borrowing money from itself. Banks, hedge funds and individual investors through their brokerage accounts will contribute to the effort as well. These entities already hold one third of U.S. debt. The Fed, which owns another 10 percent, could also increase its buying. But sooner or later domestic appetite for U.S. debt will also begin to wane, and the Treasury will find it increasingly challenging to entice domestic lenders to increase their bond holding with such meager returns. At this point, there will be no escape from raising bond yields to keep up with the paper money shoved into the market by the U.S. government. And this is when things will begin to get dicey. High interest rates will drain money away from equities and real estate markets, not to mention their derivatives, back to interest-bearing investments. This could lead to the type of market crash and mortgage crisis experienced in 2008, only this time the government will not have the same fiscal and monetary fire extinguishers it had in the previous crisis, and it will certainly not have the same international goodwill, particularly China's, which helped carry the day back then. How bad things could get is anyone's guess. All being equal, decline in the world's demand for dollars will inevitably manifest itself in a depreciated dollar relative to other currencies. A weaker dollar would make U.S. goods more competitive internationally, but it would also raise the costs of commodity and intermediate inputs, not to mention imported manufactured goods. For a consumption-driven society like America, this also means one word that many Americans have forgotten: inflation.

## The low inflation myth

"Inflation is the toxic problem with respect to the economy and markets," said former Fed Chairman Alan Greenspan. To be sure, it helps the government generate more tax revenues as wages increase. It can also cause a country's currency to devalue relative to other currencies and this makes it easier for the government to pay its debt. In other words, inflation reduces the value of the existing debt burden. But none of these are enough to offset the ugly sides of inflation. Inflation breeds a slew of problems from erosion in purchasing power to unemployment and slower growth. As happened in the last major bout of inflation, during the Nixon years, when prices rise, voters get angry and force politicians to look for quick interventionist fixes like price controls which always end in disaster. Thanks to the inflation-damping effect of globalization, which has led to lower wage pressures throughout the world, for an entire generation of Americans the scourge of high inflation is as un-relatable as Soviet-style food lines. It simply cannot happen over here. But this may soon change.

At one point or another deficits of the size the U.S. is running breed inflation. To this, even high-deficit advocates like Kelton agree: "The only potential risk with the national debt increasing over time is inflation," she said. But "to the extent you don't believe the U.S. is facing a long term inflation problem you shouldn't believe the U.S. is facing a long term debt problem."[15] This is not a minority view. Most American politicians and economists, from the left to the right, recognize the danger of inflation but they view it like Ebola, something that is out there in Africa and we certainly need to keep an eye on it, but not something we need to worry about here at home.

This complacency has been created because the U.S. government has been misleading us all to believe that inflation does not exist. But it does. The government measures inflation using two indexes. The U.S. Department of Labor's Bureau of Labor Statistics has a tool called Consumer Price Index (CPI), which is a basket of goods and services the average household consumes. The Personal Consumption Expenditure deflator, or PCE price index, is tracked by the Bureau of Economic Analysis of the U.S. Department of Commerce. The difference is that the CPI measures what households are buying while the PCE looks at what businesses are selling. Since the 1980s, U.S. inflation has been under control and over the past decade it has hovered around the two percent level. This means that, according to the government, over the past decade the cost of living should have gone up by about 20 percent. But comparing sticker prices of books, food items, health insurance, college tuition and rent from a decade ago, it appears that most prices have actually gone up by more—sometimes much more—than the government claims. In 2009 for example a daily print edition of the *New York Times* was selling at the newsstand for $2.00. Ten years later, it sells for $3.00—a 50 percent increase. It should sell for $2.44. Could it be that the cost of paper or ink has gone up way above the CPI? But wait, the exact same jump was also registered with a single New York Subway ride. A Big Mac cost $3.57 in 2009. According to the government CPI figure, it should have cost $4.37. But the actual price in 2019 is $5.58—a 55 percent increase. Even gasoline prices almost doubled despite the shale oil boom that unleashed vast amounts of made-in-America oil. We could go on and on into other household expenses from general tuition to medical care and see that most items consumed by most Americans are a lot more expensive than the bean counters in Washington would have you believe. So what's going on here?

While most of the products we consume have risen in price above and beyond the official inflation figures, the overall inflation figures remained low due to a combination of unique yet transitory developments. First, inflation indexes have benefitted from falling prices of widely used electronic equipment like televisions, phones, computers and photographic equipment that are staple products for the typical household. The reason we could benefit from cheap cell phones and tablets was the flow of cheap labor into the workforce in developing countries like China. But this flow is now slowing down and will lead to stronger wage pressures and higher prices, especially if the trade war with China escalates. Second, we also benefitted from a prolonged period of relatively low oil prices. Fuel is part of the price of almost everything we consume so when American oil producers unlocked billions of new barrels and drove down global oil prices, consumers benefitted. If not for the shale boom, oil prices would have been much higher. But this too is a transitory phenomenon. Riding on the wave of low interest rates, U.S. shale oil producers secured debt to the tune of almost $300 billion. With oil prices low and with their wells rapidly declining, many producers have been forced to restructure their debts while others are already seeking Chapter 11 bankruptcy protection. At some point, the budgetary pressures in the petrodollar dependent economies of OPEC and Russia will become intolerable, while North American production slows down, forcing prices to rebound. Third, the monetary policies implemented since the Great Recession have inflated a massive asset bubble, which have led to an astounding increase in household wealth. This means that asset prices, which are not typically reflected in the government's inflation calculations, have grown far more than consumer prices. This too is going to change once interest rates are forced upward and asset prices begin to shrink.

Bottom line, inflation does exist and will get much worse once factors like tariffs, higher oil prices and higher interest rates percolate into the economy. Statistics that misrepresent the true level of inflation give the government, policymakers and economic talking heads the justification to inculcate the mantra that inflation is nonexistent and therefore we can print more money. But once investors and foreign central bankers buying U.S. bonds conclude that real inflation is much higher than the government claims and that it is crawling upward, they will demand higher yields to compensate for the risk of losing money through inflation. This pressure could eventually force interest rates higher and higher, popping the massive asset bubbles that have been inflated for years. The implications for the dollar could be dire.

## When the music stops

The current economic conditions of perpetually low interest rates, ballooning deficits and slowing global growth on the one hand and growing pushback against the dollar on the other create an explosive mix that is often ignored by a collective sense of economic euphoria in the midst of what President Trump referred to as "the greatest economy in our Country's history."[16] It may be true that some relatively good years are still ahead of us. But the longer-term prognosis points to a perfect storm that is poised to forever alter the global financial and strategic landscape. Sooner or later, every party ends and so will the era of cheap money. When exactly and how abruptly this will happen is anybody's guess. We can predict that winter is coming but we cannot predict the first snow day. There are simply too many variables at play. When in 1996 Alan Greenspan warned about "irrational exuberance" in the markets it took another four years and an 80 percent rise in stock prices before the dot-com bubble finally burst. Furthermore, the United States is an integral part of the global system and its fate depends to a large extent on developments in other major countries which are less transparent than ours and therefore even more difficult to predict. But while there is no crystal ball to determine the future, the convergence of some general trends and trajectories point to one direction.

As baby boomers' retirement continues at a pace of about 10,000 a day, raising health and pension costs, it is expected that whoever occupies the White House in the years to come will be pushing for policies that grow, rather than shrink, the federal deficit. Defense budgets are likely to grow in response to emerging conventional and non-conventional threats from China, Russia, and the Middle East, not to mention a likely resurgence of Islamic terrorism, which has not yet perished from the earth. Republicans traditionally push for additional tax cuts and low interest rates in order to resuscitate a slowing economy as well as much needed investment in upgrading the nation's decaying infrastructure. These policies do not bode well for the deficit. At the same time, the Democratic base applies immense pressure on its leaders to implement costly social and progressive policies in the spirit of the Green New Deal. MMT economists provide the ideological justification for enlarging the deficit. And while Democrats hope to fund their expensive programs by taxing the rich, such taxation by itself can never close the fiscal gap. The result: repeated raising of the debt ceiling, government shutdowns and downgrades by credit rating agencies. And all of this assumes that no unusual exogenous event like war, terror attack or natural disaster takes place. Such events, as we learned from the past, would cause global turmoil and add hundreds of billions, if not trillions, to the deficit.

At this pace, as our national debt continues to inflate, the cost of debt servicing will become the number one expenditure of the U.S. government, crowding out domestic spending, military budgets and foreign aid. This will require the U.S. to reassess its national and international obligations, make tough choices between guns and butter, outsource its foreign policy to friends and allies and yield ground abroad to adversaries and competitors, particularly China and Russia who are eager to fill the vacuum caused by America's retreat.

Republicans and Democrats will want to keep interest rates as low as possible for as long as possible, but as the U.S. goes deeper into the red, its foreign debt holders, let alone the dollar insurgents, will become increasingly reluctant to increase their U.S. bond holdings and pressure will mount for higher bond yields. Because Treasury yields are a benchmark for U.S. consumer and business credit, interest rates on everything from corporate bonds to homeowners' mortgages will rise, likely slowing the economy. Additionally, the volume of activity in U.S. dollars will decline as more countries follow Russia and China in moving their trade to alternative currencies. Slowing demand for dollars by central banks would inevitably lead to depreciation of the greenback. This will reduce the liquidity of the dollar market and increase the effects on exchange rates of large sales or purchases of U.S. dollars. Dollar exchange rate volatility will inevitably raise transaction costs throughout the globe. The denomination of international contracts, including debt contracts, in dollars has insulated the United States economy from foreign shocks. Import prices are less affected as a result of the transaction being in dollars. But the more contracts, including in commodity trading, are inked in non-dollar currencies, the stronger the impact international shocks will have on the U.S. economy.

As the dollar weakens, U.S. goods will become more competitive abroad, but this will raise the prices of imported goods, fueling inflation well above the Fed's 2 percent target. Most Americans are unfamiliar with the 10 percent and up inflation rates of the 1970's. It is worth checking back on that period to get a taste of what may be coming. A dollar decline would exact a high price from the Chinese economy. With cash reserves of $3 trillion, much of them dollarized, every 10 percent devaluation of the dollar means a transfer of wealth of $300 billion from China to the United States. The Chinese will demand some compensation for their losses, and this will make the relations even tenser than they are today. The simmering dispute over trade is just the prelude for a much deeper conflict over technology, currency and geopolitical outreach. Washington will continue to push China to introduce market reforms and punish it for various transgressions. China, emerging from what it calls "a century of humiliation," will not budge. Eventually it will hit back—and hard—deploying some of its unconventional economic weapons including withdrawal from Treasury bond purchases. As China and other members of the dollar insurgency use U.S. Treasury buying as leverage on Washington, bond markets will become increasingly volatile. The U.S. will respond ferociously with more trade sanctions, roiling global markets, and the Fed will be frequently called to intervene in foreign exchange markets. Such a turn of events will blow winds in the sails of the de-dollarization movement, leading to stronger coordination among the insurgents and the bolstering of alternative financial mechanisms. BRICS, we predict, will become a platform on which de-dollarization efforts will concentrate. The group and its institutions will grow in numbers and influence and it will put increasing pressure on the international community, especially struggling members of the crumbling Eurozone, to consider reform of the international monetary system.

A big winner will be gold. Gold demand will spike with growing interest in an introduction of a 21$^{st}$ century gold standard, possibly supported by a gold-backed SDR or even a joint CBDC. More and more countries will repatriate their gold reserves from U.S. vaults in order to maintain full control of their reserves. Over time, the dollar will cease to be the Lingua Franca of the currency world or the hub connecting all spokes in international trade. But it will not be replaced by an existing currency. There is simply not one around to fit the role. The new monetary system will be more decentralized. Countries will increasingly conduct their bilateral trade in non-dollar currencies, more and more assets and commodities will be denominated in non-dollar currencies and central banks' reserve portfolios will be increasingly diversified away from the greenback. The result will be steady erosion in the status of the dollar as reserve currency which in turn will dampen America's fiscal credibility, prestige and prowess.

The process may be slow and steady, allowing the U.S. political system the time to adjust to the global changes, but under certain conditions it could develop into a self-reinforcing category 5 economic hurricane. Cheap money is to the U.S. economy what warm and humid air is to a hurricane. Reduced global demand for dollars means that the United States would no longer be able to print so much money to finance its deficits. But with its debts mounting, the U.S. will be forced to raise interest rates and as a result trillions of dollars will be drained from existing investments classes, bursting one by one all the bubbles that have been recklessly inflated for well over a decade by cheap and abundant money. A decade ago, the global financial crisis eliminated $60 trillion of wealth and caused painful economic contraction. The explosion of the asset bubbles that have been created since could cause far worse damage. The risk America faces is one of a toxic combination of stagnation and inflation called stagflation. Stagflation reared its ugly head in the United States in the late 1970's with the backdrop of the Arab Oil Embargo and the Cold War. Back then our debt-to-GDP ratio was around 30 percent, but today, it is over 100 percent, the highest since World War II, and it is projected to rise to 180 percent by 2050. This means that a bout of stagflation today would be far more painful than it was in the past.

A dollar decline accompanied by a period of stagflation is a particularly dangerous scenario and it could lead to war. This would not be our top concern if not for the recent deterioration of relations with China. In his book, *Destined for War: Can America and China Escape Thucydides's Trap?* Harvard University Professor Graham Allison noted that only in four of the 16 historical cases of a rising power challenging an incumbent one did imaginative statecraft avert war. In all the rest war was the result.[17] War between China and the United States may not necessarily be a conventional one in which bombers fly over Shanghai or U.S. Marines mount an amphibious landing in Hainan Island. It is more likely to be a prolonged period in which both sides hurl economic grenades in order to undermine each other's industrial bases, research centers and financial markets, using currency manipulations, cyber weapons, embargoes and other tools of economic warfare. Like the Cold War, such a war will be long and costly, a war that is decided by points, not by knockout. The problem with such a war between the world's two largest economies, together contributing fully half of the world's growth, is that it will eventually result in economic decoupling as more and more businesses reroute their supply chains. The trade feud, fierce competition over technology, mounting market barriers, currency wars and the destruction of people-to-people relations will all make U.S.-China relations prohibitive, sundering the connective tissues that have held the two economies together since the 1990s.

## Unexpecteds to the rescue?

There is another scenario, a much brighter one in which the dollar wins a second life thanks to the misfortunes of its competitors. For all of its gathering might, the dollar insurgency suffers from a serious weakness: all of its lead members—Russia, Europe and China—are more economically vulnerable than the United States. More than five years after the imposition of international sanctions, Russia's economy is sputtering and the Russian people are becoming fed up with the Kremlin's empty promises of economic revival. Oil prices remain too low to offset the decline in Russia's internal investments in infrastructure and government services, and Putin's popularity is sinking. The Russian people are known for their high pain tolerance but at some point they too could lose faith in Putin's leadership and storm the Kremlin as they have done several times in the past.

Europe's future is also dim. The pressures in the Eurozone are real, acute and escalating. All of Europe's major economies are either in recession or on the brink of one, the banking system is failing and the European electorate is increasingly shifting toward nationalism. A collapse of the Eurozone is no longer a fictional scenario. If it happens, European economies would go back to their erstwhile currencies and central bankers would be flocking to the safe(r) haven of the dollar.

Then there is the biggest enigma of all—China. China's economic growth is decelerating; its population is aging; its internal debt has grown to ominous proportions and its banks are fiscal black holes. China may not be as interconnected with other financial powerhouses like the United States and Europe, but turmoil in its economy would reverberate across global markets. In the event of a crisis, the CPC would have to tap into its sovereign funds and cash reserves to recapitalize its banks. It would also take immediate measures to devalue the yuan in order to reboot the country's export driven economy. Such actions would obviously impact the dollar. An economic crisis in China may cause the Chinese to hit the brakes on additional U.S. bond buying, but it would also mean a run by the rest of the concerned world to the dollar and U.S. bonds.

Major political or economic upheaval in China, Russia, Europe or any combination of the three will send the de-dollarization movement into deep freeze, and this could re-solidify the dollar's role of reserve currency for many years to come. As George Soros correctly pointed out: "The dollar is the weakest currency except for all the others."[18] That said, sitting on our hands waiting for our rivals and competitors to falter should not be our work plan. We must take a sober look at our future, comprehend the risks and realize that the dollar is not divinely ordained as the reserve currency. Its status must be protected like any other element of our national power.

# 8 TOWARD A CURRENCY PROTECTION STRATEGY

*Economic security is national security.*
*President Donald J. Trump, November 2017*

After the First World War, John Maynard Keynes attended the Paris Peace Conference of 1919 as a delegate of the British Treasury. Under the impression of the historic conference and the resulting Treaty of Versailles, he published his international bestseller *The Economic Consequences of the Peace,* an acclaimed critique of the Treaty of Versailles and in particular the harsh terms imposed on Germany. Keynes believed that the seeds sown in Versailles would result in the financial collapse of Germany and subsequently economic chaos throughout Europe and the world. Tucked in the book is a frequently cited quote by Vladimir Ilyich Lenin saying that "the best way to destroy the capitalist system [is] to debauch the currency." Lenin, who dedicated his life to the destruction of capitalism, understood the centrality of money as a reliable store of value in a capitalistic society. To break what he viewed as a morally flawed social order and class differences, the Bolshevik leader believed in the destruction of money through devaluation and hyperinflation. If markets are flooded with notes with high face value but without guarantee of purchasing value, people will cease to hoard them and the system on which they stand would collapse. Keynes did not subscribe to Lenin's radical view on money, but he foresaw Lenin's vision of monetary destruction materializing in Germany. He concluded that an imposed upon political solution based on coercion and vindictiveness, like the one crafted in Versailles, would not hold. In the years that followed, he witnessed hyperinflation consuming what was left of the Weimar Republic, giving rise to Nazism and its horrible repercussions. It was only in 1944 in Bretton Woods that Keynes' elevated status allowed him to lead the world to adopt the dollar-based financial architecture that has governed the global financial system ever since.

We write this book exactly 100 years after Versailles, and the world again seems to be sliding into disarray. The international trade system is facing unprecedented strains; old alliances are being fragmented while new ones are being created; currency wars, tariffs and embargoes are back in fashion; global institutions and treaties are losing their teeth; and a growing uneasiness about the resilience of the global monetary system is surfacing. To top it off, socialism is rearing its head again in of all places the bastion of capitalism, the United States, in what could be a titanic battle of ideas.

Many Americans, basking in their swelling stock portfolios, are paying little attention to these new forces, not least to the pushback against the U.S.-dominated financial system. There is no subtle way to say it: the world is becoming fed up with America's exorbitant privilege and is growingly eager to move from a system based on a one-size-fits-all unit of settlement to a multipolar monetary system which is more reflective of the 21$^{st}$ century international balance of power. The evidence for this trend is clear, abundant and growing. The greenback's share of global central bank reserves is on a steady decline; a growing portion of global trade is shifting from dollars to alternative currencies; mechanisms like the SWIFT network and the petrodollar system, which granted the United States strategic advantages over the past half century, are gradually being challenged by new and de-dollarized alternatives; and new multinational organizations are rising with the stated goal of balancing, if not replacing, U.S.-led institutions and instruments of power. All of these trends are diminishing the world's demand for the dollar and its derivatives at a time U.S. borrowing needs are rising like never before. This is a train wreck in the making.

Due to the nascent nature of the dollar insurgency and the internal challenges facing each of its members, it is too early to determine the pace, intensity and likelihood of success of the effort to dethrone the dollar. Nor can we predict with confidence what a new multipolar monetary landscape might look like. Will the dollar continue to be a safe haven for investors? Will China continue its growth momentum and succeed in mounting a real challenge to U.S. preeminence? Will the Eurozone survive? Will the Middle East turn a corner? All of these unknowns will have a deep impact on the future of the greenback. Some positive, others negative. What is safer to predict is that to the degree a new system eventually takes hold, it will no longer be connected to the economic conditions and sovereign interests of the United States or any other single country for that matter. No more exorbitant privilege. The successor system will be more reflective of the multipolar nature of our new world, sharing power with China, India, Brazil, Nigeria, Indonesia and other emerging economic powerhouses.

Americans should not assume that the forces of de-dollarization will fade away or that the pushback against both its leadership, and by extension its currency, will ease. We may be only in the beginning of a protracted and intensifying process. This should only cause us to lend more urgency to staying on top of the race for the future of the monetary system. Our response should be systemic, disciplined and bipartisan. It should stem from the understanding that the dollar's special status is the most important element of our national greatness and that it should be protected like any other element of our national infrastructure—with defense mechanisms, budgets and close supervision by the executive and legislative branches. The United States has a National Strategy for Counterterrorism, a National Cyber Strategy, a National Strategy for Homeland Security, a National Infrastructure Protection Plan and numerous agencies and policies worrying about nuclear safety and the protection of our nuclear arsenal. But we do not have a currency protection strategy. Nor do we have the intelligence apparatus needed to assess the risk on an ongoing basis or a proper inter-agency process to devise and execute a defense strategy. Most Americans take the dollar's global reserve currency status for granted. This can no longer be the case. It is time to fight for it.

Our proposed strategy to defend the dollar consists of four pillars.

First, we must understand the problem and create the necessary mechanisms to assess and mitigate the risks. Without proper understanding of the threat, it will be impossible to master the resources and political support necessary for effective defense plan. This means retooling our Washington bureaucracy, both intellectually and operationally, in such a way that allows the government to protect the hegemony of our currency. For decades, Washington's foreign policy establishment has been accustomed to seeing the world through a geopolitical prism. Going forward, our challenges will be more about geo-economics than geopolitics, and our foreign policy experts, diplomats and politicians must become well versed in the language, theory and practice of economic statecraft and geo-economics - the art that strategist Edward Luttwak once defined as "the logic of conflict in the grammar of commerce."

Second, we must do all we can to nip the nascent problem in the bud - while we still can. We are in the early stage of de-dollarization, "Stage I" cancer if you will. This problem is not going away, and waiting it out is not an option. This pillar entails real changes in America's international behavior and priorities—both in style and in substance. We must recognize the long-term ramifications of our current economic statecraft and our trigger-happiness when it comes to the use of financial coercion against other countries, especially our closest allies. The more we condition our financial system on adherence to U.S. foreign policy, the more the risk of migration to other currencies and other financial systems. We must reexamine our automated use of sanctions as the go-to element in our foreign relations. There are simply too many countries under U.S. sanctions with little evidence the sanctions have brought about meaningful behavioral change. For sanctions to succeed there must always be broad international support, rigorous execution, and reliable expectations by the sanctioned country that behavioral change will be rewarded with relief. If we cannot guarantee all three at the get-go, it is better not to start the journey. We must also nip in the bud our recent tendency to spoil relations with allies, which have been built over decades and centuries, for some short-term financial or diplomatic gains. After our military and the power of the dollar, our alliance system is the most valuable asset we have and it is central to maintaining our superpower status. If we allow our alliances to falter, we will eventually lose the preeminence of the dollar and shortly after our ability to finance our military.

Third, and perhaps most important, we must deal with the underlying issues that cause the world's eroding faith in our currency, top among them: our out-of-control deficits and the growing sense that the United States is using the dollar system to advance its own domestic economy at the expense of the rest of the world.

Many countries are growing to realize that they are subsidizing the American dream while their own dreams have turned into nightmares. What used to be widely accepted no longer is. If we fail to put our fiscal house in order, control our excessive spending and make real efforts to reduce our debt, we will ultimately face financial ruin. We must resist the temptation of falling in love with voodoo economic theories like the MMT on the left and clarion calls to increase spending while cutting taxes from the right. These will only exacerbate an already unsustainable debt burden. We do not propose an economically suffocating austerity. What is needed is a combination of fiscal discipline and policies that foster long-term growth.

We must also reassess our approach toward China. America is addicted to debt and at the same time seems hell-bent on picking every possible fight with its number one trading partner and a major debt holder. We cannot have it both ways. To be sure, China's rise is a huge strategic challenge for the United States and President Trump's call for readjustments in our relations with Beijing is warranted, but the recent wave of China hysteria that has engulfed Washington in recent years is unfocused, wrongheaded and self-defeating. China's population is four times our own and the Chinese people have bought hook, line, and sinker the dream of wealth accumulation. The United States cannot halt China's rise and its combative approach will only produce deep hostility among the Chinese people and wreak havoc in the international system, forcing many of our allies desperately dependent on China's largesse to drift away from the United States. China's rise must be managed, but it should not be sabotaged. China must be treated as a great power and while we may not like everything about the Chinese form of governance (they too are not terribly impressed by ours), we must resist reckless ideas about regime change and other experiments in social engineering on a country comprised of a fifth of humanity. We must also avoid falling into the mental trap of seeing the world through a zero-sum prism in which China's rise necessarily comes at our expense. Sometimes this will be the case, but in many other ways China's foreign investments, infrastructure and connectivity projects could actually benefit the United States, offering the world's economically depressed and disconnected communities access to markets, America's included. China's rise should not be a call-to-arms but a wakeup call for us to stop whining, put on our running shoes, lose some weight and work harder to remain number one. As Trump once said: "I want the United States to win through competition, not by blocking out currently more advanced technologies."[1]

The fourth element of our strategy is winning the future. The third decade of the 21st century will herald the maturation of several key technologies that will redefine the future of humanity. Artificial intelligence, machine learning, internet of things based on fifth (5G) and sixth (6G) generation decentralized web, quantum computing, robotics, autonomous transportation and others will bring about what Klaus Schwab called the Fourth Industrial Revolution which will change every aspect of our social and economic behavior.[2] These breakthroughs will be augmented by scientific revolutions in biomedicine, genetic engineering and other life sciences. These, in turn, could eradicate diseases like cancer and Alzheimer's and extend overall life expectancy, but they will also upend our entire legacy economic system and transform our relationship with the concepts of "work" and "retirement." Exactly how all these elements will shape our future and the role of government in our lives is a topic for another book. What we dare predict is that the monetary system will not remain untouched by all of those developments.

Indeed, it is hard to see the digitized economy of the information era continuing to run on Yuan Dynasty paper money served over the counters of a 15th century institution called the "bank." If the information revolution taught us anything, it is that those who draw the contour lines and set industry standards end up commanding the space. The same is true for financial technologies. To win the future, the United States must maintain its leadership in financial innovation, especially in Blockchain-based settlement mechanisms, digital currencies, peer-to-peer payment platforms and crowd-lending. This way it can ensure that it is not blindsided by the emergence of a new financial mechanism that negates U.S. interests.

Here is the strategy in detail.

## Understand the problem

- **Monitor de-dollarization efforts and their impact.** De-dollarization is a slow moving trend comprised of numerous and seemingly disassociated actions and policies spanning multiple geographies and markets. It is not easy to see the connections and interplays between the various players, events and micro-trends. In order to assess the risk, it is important to establish a centralized collection and monitoring mechanism within the U.S. government to provide decision makers with an accurate and current picture of de-dollarization efforts worldwide and the risks they pose.

- **Assign a point person in charge of the issue.** The vastness of the government on the one hand and the multi-disciplinary nature of the problem on the other create difficulties in forming an all-of-government response to long-term challenges. This national security challenge merits a designated office within the White House apparatus, a dollar czar if you will, that would assume responsibility for the issue and manage an inter-agency process with officials from the National Security Council, National Economic Council,

Treasury, Commerce, Justice and State Departments as well as the intelligence community.

- **Strengthen foreign economic intelligence gathering on matters related to de-dollarization.** Much of the information gathering on the inner working of the de-dollarization effort can be obtained through open source financial market analysis. However, some of the information can only be obtained through intelligence work. This includes the tracking of secret movements of precious metals, covert de-dollarization policies, oil and other commodities trading, trends in digital currencies technology adoption and policies and investment decisions of foreign countries in sectors and companies relevant to de-dollarization. The Director of National Intelligence should direct the National Intelligence Council (NIC) to research and author a National Intelligence Estimate on foreign governments' efforts to undermine the dollar and to maintain permanent in-house expertise on the subject.

- **Educate Congress.** Congress should hold periodic hearings on de-dollarization and direct the Treasury Department to produce a bi-annual report on global de-dollarization efforts. Congress should also review policies that are likely to accelerate the de-dollarization effort and undermine the preeminence of the U.S. financial system and address them through policies and legislation.

- **Track global gold movements.** Feeling overly exposed to the dollar and seeking to take advantage of relatively low gold prices, many central banks are looking to diversify away from the dollar and add the yellow metal to their reserves. In all probability, any competing currency to the dollar would be backed by gold and possibly other precious metals. In order to anticipate such changes, the United States should always maintain an accurate picture of gold reserves and movements. Many of the movements can be tracked in open market transactions, but large volumes of gold are also shipped around the globe in secrecy. The more accurate the accounting of gold is, the easier it will be to anticipate changes in monetary conditions. The intelligence community should be tasked with providing an ongoing assessment.

- **Monitor non-dollarized oil/commodities trading.** The Department of Energy and the Intelligence Community should keep track of global oil and commodity movements and provide ongoing assessment of non-dollar transactions in order to determine changing market conditions. Washington should also communicate to the government of Saudi Arabia that the U.S. commitment to the security of the House of Saud will be contingent on Saudi protection of the petrodollar system.

- **Keep an eye on BRICS.** The BRICS mechanism has been discounted by many policymakers for lacking organization and teeth. Ten years after its formation, this platform is poised to become the political and economic fertile ground on which a new monetary system can grow. The United States is not and will not be a BRICS member but it should observe and monitor from afar BRICS decisions and policy directions. It should also use its good relations with India and Brazil to influence these two BRICS members to resist turning the group into an anti-dollar alliance. The transition from BRICS to BRICS+ should be closely monitored, and the U.S. government should constantly evaluate the potential implications of BRICS expansion.

## Stem the tide

- **Reassess U.S. financial coercive measures with the understanding the U.S. has overplayed its hand.** Viewed singularly, all U.S. sanctions programs have legal, moral and in most cases geopolitical merits. However, the accumulation of so many sanctions and coercive measures is diluting their effectiveness. Beyond a certain point, more is less. The practice of secondary sanctions also merits a second thought. Secondary sanctions may be effective in insulating and mounting pressure on the sanctioned entity, but they bear a considerable hidden cost in terms of world sentiment toward the United States. Unilateral secondary sanctions are an assault on third party state sovereignty, and the cost of their overuse could outweigh their benefits. The U.S. government and Congress should reassess its entire sanctions program. Sanctions should be used more judiciously and more surgically or else they will only serve to prod the revisionists to initiate structural changes in the global financial system that over time could provide a viable alternative to more and more countries and entities within the sanction busting community. Congress and the executive branch should also adopt a process by which new sanctions contemplated are assessed not only for their potential benefits but also for their potential costs and unintended consequences. Sanctions should not be open ended but rather imposed for a limited period of time with an option for extension. Their cost and impact should be assessed at periodic intervals thereafter. Additionally, the U.S. should be extra scrupulous when imposing sanctions on major powers like China or Russia as opposed to second and third tier powers whose retaliation would be of little consequence to the United States. As U.S.-China and U.S.-Russia relations are moving toward confrontation, the temptation to punish China and Russia with more and more sanctions will become increasingly difficult to resist. But if we learned anything from the trade feud of 2017-2019, it is that great powers with a history of humiliation do not turn the other cheek when hit. They react badly to economic coercion and other measures they deem humiliating. It should therefore be taken as a given that U.S. sanctions on China and Russia—for whatever reason—will be swiftly answered by Beijing and Moscow with equally painful retaliation.

- **Harmonize law enforcement efforts with national security/economic security.** The Treasury and Justice Departments often use coercive economic measures against countries, foreign corporations and foreign individuals for not following U.S. law and punish them just because they can. This is viewed by many as a fundamental violation of the principle of sovereignty in international affairs. The problem is that administration officials doing their job to the best of their ability are not always fully aware of the broad repercussions of their actions on America's long-term strategic interests. A classic example was the arrest in Canada of Huawei's CFO Meng Wanzhou per the extradition request of the Justice Department. It may be that from a pure legal perspective the indictment had merit, but the cost of pursuing justice was much higher than anticipated. The arrest sent China-Canada relations into a tailspin, prompting retaliatory arrests of Canadian citizens in China and punitive measures against Canadian farm exports to China. This created deep anger in Canada against the United States for dragging it into a great power rivalry. Coming in the midst of high-stakes U.S.-China trade negotiations, the arrest also soured the atmosphere in the talks, causing many uninvolved constituencies unnecessary harm. The Meng saga has inflicted collateral damage on so many innocent bystanders, one must ask if any legal victory is a Pyrrhic one. The administration must adopt a more rigorous assessment process when applying extra-territorial jurisdiction considering the potential harm to U.S. interests and to those of its allies, as well as to the long-term reactions of affected entities. Sometimes, it is better to be wise than just.

- **Reassess FATCA.** Toward the tenth anniversary of FATCA's enactment, Congress should conduct a thorough cost-benefit analysis of this controversial law. The review should assess the federal revenue raised as a result of the law as well as its national security benefits versus the cost of compliance and the discriminatory treatment against U.S. expatriates who bear the high compliance costs at a time they enjoy no U.S. government benefits. Congress should direct the State Department to provide data on the role FATCA plays in the decision of more than 5,000 U.S. citizens to renounce their citizenship annually. Many of them do not state the true reason for their decision in their farewell interviews in U.S. embassies abroad for fear of government harassment. The State Department should therefore commission a survey among former U.S. citizens, who renounced their citizenship over the past decade to determine the impact of FATCA on their decision.

- **Be smart on SWIFT.** SWIFT is not an American institution, but as recent history shows it is one that is heavily influenced by Washington. Recently, Washington has been tempted to assert its will on SWIFT and use it as an instrument in its coercive financial policies. This practice may be hard to resist in trying to achieve short-term foreign policy goals. But strong arming SWIFT will intensify the efforts by China and Russia to push their alternative systems and perhaps even merge them into one powerful platform. This will have a negative and lasting impact on SWIFT, which over the long-term weakens the U.S. ability to monitor financial transactions. The United States should therefore generally avoid coercing SWIFT and its board and employees. This option should be reserved for very special circumstances.

- **Restore and strengthen the U.S. alliance system and prevent new recruits from joining the dollar insurgency.** America's relationships with traditional allies have undergone severe strains in recent years, leaving many countries to wonder if the United States is still a trusted ally. Concerns about U.S. commitment to the old order have led many countries to seek alternative relations and security alliances. Continuous disintegration of America's alliance system will catalyze further abandonment of the dollar system. At this point the connective tissues of the U.S. alliance system are still repairable—but not for much longer. Europe's dire economic conditions will make it more susceptible to drift toward China and accept terms of trade that further de-dollarization. While the Trump administration had some good reasons to shake up the State Department and change its organizational culture, the White House's go-it-alone style, its dismissive approach toward traditional diplomacy and multilateralism and the hollowing out of the U.S. diplomatic corps has resulted in some foreign policy bankruptcies that have left the U.S. weakened abroad. This course needs to be corrected.

## Address the macro

- **Get serious about the national debt.** Much lip service has been paid to the need to address America's mounting debt. But short-term political expediencies have precluded Washington from tackling this existential matter in any meaningful way. With few exceptions, both Republicans and Democrats have abdicated their commitment to fiscal discipline. Former Fed Chairman Alan Greenspan summed up the situation: "Despite the huge increase that we've seen in the debt, nothing is happening. People are behaving like it's a terrible thing, but [say] 'I want a little more.'"[3] It is easy to kick the can down the road and pass the problem to the next generation, but this is not how a country wins the future. Congress and the administration should put the nation's debt on a stable course, setting a long-term goal of reining in the debt to a target of no more than 60 percent of GDP by 2050. Congress must preserve the Pay As You GO (PAYGO) mechanism that requires the Office of Management and Budget (OMB) to offset the cost of deficit-increasing legislation by forcing across-the-board cuts in federal mandatory spending. But because four categories — Social Security, Medicare and Medicaid, defense, and interest payments on the debt—account for more than two-thirds of all spending, reining in the debt can no longer be achieved exclusively though budget cuts that ignore the first three. There is no escape from either deeply cutting spending in these categories or else seeking more revenues. How much to cut, whom to tax and by how much is beyond the purview of this book. But it is important to remember that overly aggressive corrections on either taxation or spending reduction could be detrimental to our future in as far as they undermine new public investment in human and physical capital that is essential for future economic growth. The debate will be fierce and the choices are tough, but it is important to understand that failure to stabilize our fiscal situation will inescapably usher in dire consequences for the dollar that must not be ignored.

- **Respect the Fed's independence.** The Fed plays a critical role in shaping the future of the dollar. Its role, as its ninth and longest-serving chairman William McChesney Martin Jr. famously defined, is "to take away the punch bowl just as the party gets going" even at the risk of being the most unpopular person in the room. Chairman Jerome Powell acknowledged that the "federal government's debt is on an unsustainable path." Even though he stated that the "non-sustainability of the U.S. federal government isn't really something that plays into the medium term that is relevant to our policy decisions," Powell understands that the responsibility of the Fed in protecting the economy is to refill the monetary fire extinguishers in preparation for the next financial crisis.[4] This means raising interest rates to a reasonable level even at the risk of incurring the White House's wrath. After raising rates by one percent in total over four hikes in 2018, Powell came under unprecedented attack by President Trump with implicit threats to fire the chairman, calling the Fed "crazy" and "very destructive."[5] Trump also contemplated firing Powell, and when this proved impossible he tried to politicize the Fed by replacing what he called "not my people" board members with loyalists. Powell is not the first Fed chairman to come under fire for sacrificing short-term political expediencies in favor of the long-term health of the economy. What is unprecedented is the degree of hostility exhibited by Trump. Such actions undermine the Fed's credibility and independence in the eyes of the American people, let alone international central bankers who are regularly making decisions about the composition of their foreign exchange reserves. Furthermore, it seems gratuitous that as the U.S. government is criticizing other countries for manipulating their currencies and is even threatening punitive action against them, it attacks its own central bank for not doing the same. The Fed should be left alone to determine the monetary policies that best serve the country and the world. It is not part of one president or another's reelection committee.

- **Chill out on trade deficits until the rest of our fiscal house is in order.** Trade deficits are a byproduct of a strong economy. People buy more imported good because they have more disposable income. The money we send overseas for these goods essentially enables other countries to buy our debt. Without a trade deficit, there will be a weaker incentive for foreign creditors to buy U.S. Treasuries and the U.S. government will lack the funds needed for social programs and national defense. A more forgiving approach toward trade deficits should not be confused with acceptance of other countries' unfair trade practices. Those should be fought against vigorously. But we should not forget that trade deficits are the fuel that have allowed successive administrations to run loose fiscal policies.

- **Hold serious and frank talks with America's top lenders about the U.S. future lending needs and patterns.** Foreign creditors are increasingly anxious about the growth trajectory of U.S. debt. They realize that continuous growth in U.S. obligations means they will be put under pressure to buy more and more U.S. debt at a time their economies are facing serious challenges. Not addressing the issue does not make it go away. The U.S. should openly discuss its future needs with its major economic partners, especially China and Japan, assessing its needs and expectations from each lender. Such conversations should take place at not only at the level of central banks but also at top leadership level. Such frankness is needed as it would give American policymakers a better sense of what could be realistically expected from foreign lenders and hence how much money would have to be raised domestically.

- **Support developing nations' ambitions to bolster their representation in international forums.** The U.S. stood alone in its opposition to the Asian Infrastructure Investment Bank and was the last to approve—reluctantly—long-awaited IMF reforms to give emerging economies a greater say in how the IMF is managed. This opposition to the inevitable proved to be self-defeating. The United States should recognize the aspirations of emerging economies for fairer representation in the IMF and the

World Bank in par with their economic weight. A failure to empathize with the needs and aspirations of the emerging economies will only force them to seek structural solutions, which in the long run will make the United States weaker.

- **Support the creation of an Asian energy market and benchmarks.** The Asian crude oil market is due for a structural transformation as major Asian buyers become more involved in price setting. For the time being, Asia is not sufficiently united to agree on a crude benchmark that is priced in any of the Asian currencies. This may change in the future as China bolsters its dominance over the Asia-Pacific region, its currency becomes sufficiently internationalized, and its demand for energy eclipses all other Asian economies. At that point, China will want the Asian benchmark to be priced in yuan. This means it is in America's interest to get in front of this situation and facilitate today the creation of a dollar-denominated Asian benchmark. Once such a benchmark is formed, it is likely to remain in place ensuring Asian energy trading remains dollarized.

- **Rethink the strategy toward China and its Belt and Road.** Washington's approach toward China has shifted dramatically during the Trump presidency. China is no longer viewed as an economic partner but as a geopolitical rival and an economic competitor that America must defeat in order to ensure its continued global hegemony. The Belt and Road, which was treated with indifference and skepticism by the Obama administration, is viewed today as a strategic ploy to expand China's economic and political influence. The prevailing view in Washington is that the BRI should be derailed and disrupted. To make its case against the BRI, the administration has invoked "opaque financing practices, poor governance and disregard for internationally accepted norms." To be sure, the plan contains projects that could, under some circumstances, undercut U.S. interests. But a close examination of it reveals that the United States has much to gain from it. Increased prosperity in the developing world will enable more consumers to demand American goods and services. U.S. engineering, construction, and equipment-manufacturing companies could win lucrative contracts, and U.S. defense and cybersecurity companies can help protect critical infrastructure worldwide. With more energy terminals, pipelines, storage facilities, and free-trade zones constructed around the world, the U.S. energy industry could enjoy more destinations for its oil, gas and coal. And with 80 percent of the people in the developing world not connected to the internet, American tech companies like Google, Amazon and Facebook can win numerous new users as more people become connected to the World Wide Web via energy and communication infrastructure. The United States should not root for the BRI's failure. Such a failure would no doubt be a blow to China's prestige, but it might hurt the United States in more than one way. The reason is that as China's cash reserves dwindle, there will be less money available for Beijing to continue to finance U.S. debt, and this will put significant strain on the U.S. government to meet its budgetary obligations. BRI's failure would depress the Chinese economy in ways that will be felt throughout the global economy. In the end, China is offering emerging countries essential infrastructures that are critical for their economic growth. This support is unmatched by the United States which is clearly unwilling (and frankly unable) to invest the resources to rival China as the world's leader in financing and executing infrastructure projects. Many countries find themselves torn between their affinity for the U.S.-led global order and their immediate financial needs, which China is willing to fulfill. As the global economy slows down and the need for infrastructure investment grows, more and more countries will gravitate toward China for solutions. So far, Washington's snub and criticism of the BRI has fallen on deaf ears. The 2017 BRI forum drew 29 heads of state; the 2019 forum welcomed 37. For all the reservations the United States might harbor about the rise of China and the BRI, it must accept the reality is that the project is moving forward with or without its participation. The United States faces two options: stay on the sidelines and continue to play the role of spoiler while witnessing its allies gravitating toward China or find ways to live with the BRI and even benefit from it. Selective yet constructive participation in the BRI will position the United States as a willing and pragmatic team player—rather than a spoiler—while also allowing it sufficient flexibility. It will also allow it to ensure from within that the BRI is not used as a platform to advance China's de-dollarization agenda.[6]

## Win the future

- **When it's time to rebuild the Middle East, make sure it's done in dollars.** Since 2011, the Middle East has been in a state of chaos with countries like Libya, Syria, Yemen and Iraq, all of them oil producing countries, reaching a state of collapse. It is expected that in the coming years these countries will emerge from the ashes and begin the process of national reconstruction. The rebuilding will require international cooperation and the investment of hundreds of billions of dollars, and much of the money will come from these countries' oil. Due to China's comparative advantage on all things related to infrastructure, Beijing is likely to be eager to incorporate the reconstruction project into the BRI framework. As part of its effort to internationalize the use of the yuan, China will try to initiate oil-for-infrastructure barter deals that will leave the dollar out of what could become the biggest post-war reconstruction effort since World War II. To protect the dollar' status, Washington must ensure that the project is not used to advance the de-dollarization effort. Washington should ensure that the multilateral development institutions in which it plays a leadership role are fully integrated in the effort and push for oil sales to be conducted in the most transparent way.

- **Stay ahead of the curve on CBDC.** The global battle for digital supremacy cannot neglect the currency space. To maintain its leadership role in the global financial system, the United States must regularly assess how innovations in the cryptocurrency and distributed ledger technology space may impact the U.S. financial system. The government must also develop a nation-wide plan for leading the world in the development and adoption of those technologies and others that can underpin the future monetary system. Ceding the advantage to its competitors will allow them to perfect the building blocks of the future and set global standards for emerging technologies. The United States must also avoid a "Sputnik moment" when a foreign country or a group of countries issues the first CBDC.

Notwithstanding the challenges of cryptocurrencies discussed before, the United States must insist on remaining an innovation center in the field of technologies that will enable future digital currencies to become reserve currencies. The American bank JP Morgan has already announced plans to launch a permissioned Blockchain-based digital coin, JPM Coin, pegged to the U.S. dollar, making it the first cryptocurrency backed by a major bank.[7] Facebook's Libra, once launched, could also change the global monetary architecture. The U.S. government should set rules and regulations for such currencies and conduct research and pilots toward development of a national dollar-backed digital currency. The United States cannot afford to be the second great power to issue a CBCD.

# EPILOGUE

USD is still the dominant reserve currency.
*U.S. Department of Treasury, 2019*[1]

The word "still" is used to convey a certain continuity of state up to and including the present. Its use often implies doubt that the future will be the continuation of the present. Is this why someone at the Department of Treasury chose to use this word in a 2019 official document reaffirming the transitory nature of the supremacy of the dollar? It would be an encouraging sign if the choice of the word "still" had been deliberate. It would mean that within the U.S. government there are those who have taken note of the trends described in this book and who are sufficiently aware of the global changes which could make the future so much different from the present. But we cannot count on that. Humans who live in times of great changes struggle to form a clear picture of the future. We are inundated with information and are generally ill equipped to grasp the convergence of so many economic, political, social and technological changes that are happening before our eyes and the way they all reinforce each other. So unique is our time that even history is no longer a reliable guide to the future. Think about it: This is the first time in human history in which life expectancy is long enough to enable four consecutive generations—Baby Boomers, Generation X, Millennials and Generation Z—which are so distinctly different from each other on matters of values, ethics, race, gender, attitudes and technological skills, to coexist and compete with each other over resources and priorities. No wonder our domestic and international discourse is so cacophonic, and as a result some really big stories miss our attention. The story of the challenge to the dollar as reserve currency is one of them. It is easy to miss. It is slow moving; it has to do with economic and financial jargon most people are not familiar with; and it is all happening at a time of economic glee, when most Americans believe the economy is in good shape. But as this book argues, far from the eye, a grand scheme is being hatched to rob America from its main instrument of power. And while this effort is still subterranean and may remain so for some years to come, when it surfaces it will do so with full force. By then it will be too late to turn the tide. Whether or not the trend is reversible depends mainly on America's ability to command respect and trust abroad while exercising foresight and discipline at home. We are still optimistic about the former, much less so about the latter.

The good news for America is that there is no great power out there that can offer a better alternative to our rules-based democratic system. This gives the United States an opening to regain its leadership status, to restore it friendships and to stem other nations' exodus to the opposite camp. But for this to happen, we must abandon the pathway of ignoring and demoralizing allies, promoting jingoism and engaging in wholesale wrecking of global institutions and covenants unless—and only unless—we are ready to offer and bring to life better ones. And while we advance our own greatness, we must also respect the right of other rising powers to be great as well, even if their greatness is achieved through political means that are not to our liking. This means, among other things, allowing some economic and geopolitical breathing room, without which conflict is inescapable.

When it comes to the other prerequisite of ensuring our financial supremacy, putting our own fiscal house in order, it is difficult to be optimistic. The American political system is fractured and increasingly dysfunctional. Deep partisanship, generational and racial conflicts and the return of the ism's—socialism and nationalism—to mainstream politics are turning the name "United States" into an oxymoron. Debt accumulation has become our only means of keeping everyone more or less content. The road America has taken in a single decade from Tea Party to *The Deficit Myth* is disturbing. It reflects a change in values, from an imperative of living within one's means to a collective sense that living at other nations' expense, or at the expense of future generations, is tolerable, if not virtuous. It will take remarkable and brave peacetime leadership to usher America back to fiscal responsibility. But can such leadership emerge in a political system burdened by divisiveness, virtue signaling and simplistic solutions to complex problems?

From the debt trap America is already in there are only three ways out. The first is a global financial crisis of epic proportions followed by years of austerity, contraction and general misery after which the debt is somehow restructured. The second is the greatest reset button of all called war, which enables debtors and lenders, exhausted from years of communal bloodletting, to renegotiate the terms of their debt and restart all over again. And because most of America's foreign debtors as well as its main competitors are in Asia, it is there where the seeds of such war are likely to germinate. The third and the only positive scenario is a renaissance-like period of technological and societal advancement which causes dramatic improvement in human productivity that can in turn generate prolonged high growth rates sufficient to balance government debts and shrink national debts. Human history has examples of each of these scenarios. For the third to take place we must own the future through entrepreneurship, research and innovation. Are we up to it?

The story of the dollar is a corollary to the story of America. In other words, it will not be the dollar's decline that will herald America's decline but the other way around. The dollar is the barometer of the world's approval of American leadership. Should America snap back from its present funk, the dollar house will continue to stand. If it continues to consume itself from within, the dollar's fate will echo the fate of all the erstwhile reserve currencies of bygone empires. Which course will America take? The rest of the world will be watching our choices. As American poet Henry Wadsworth Longfellow wrote:

*Humanity with all its fears,*
*With all the hopes of future years,*
*Is hanging breathless on thy fate!*

# ABOUT THE AUTHORS

Gal Luft and Anne Korin are co-directors of the Institute for the Analysis of Global Security, a Washington based think tank focused on energy, security, and economic trends. They are also senior advisers to the United States Energy Security Council, a cabinet level extra-governmental advisory committee. Their previous books include *Energy Security Challenges for the 21st Century* (2009), *Turning Oil into Salt: Energy Independence through Fuel Choice* (2009) and *Petropoly: The Collapse of America's Energy Security Paradigm* (2012).

For updates on the subject of this book visit dedollarization.org
For readers' comments and suggestions contact
info@dedollarization.org

# ENDNOTES

## Prologue

[1] The debate about the future of the dollar has been the topic of numerous books and articles reflecting the opinions of optimists like Jeffrey A. Frankel, "Still the Lingua Franca: The Exaggerated Death of the Dollar," *Foreign Affairs*, July/August 1995, https://www.foreignaffairs.com/articles/united-states/1995-07-01/still-lingua-franca-exaggerated-death-dollar, Barry Eichengreen, *Exorbitant Privilege: The Rise and Fall of the Dollar and the Future of the Dollar*, (Oxford: Oxford University Press 2012). On the pessimist range of the spectrum one can notably find James Rickards, *The Death of Money: The Coming Collapse of the International Monetary System*, (New York, Portfolio Penguin, 2014), Richard Duncan, *The Dollar Crisis: Causes, Consequences and Cures*, (Wiley, 2011).

[2] "Is the dollar's 'exorbitant privilege' coming to an end?" JP Morgan note to investors, July 10, 2019, https://privatebank.jpmorgan.com/gl/en/insights/investing/is-the-dollar-s-exorbitant-privilege-coming-to-an-end

## Introduction. America First and the rise of the rest

[1] Ronald I. McKinnon, "The World Dollar Standard and Globalization New Rules for the Game?," Stanford University, September 2005, http://citeseerx.ist.psu.edu/viewdoc/download?doi=10.1.1.514.3563&rep=rep1&type=pdf

2   Paul Kennedy, *The Rise and Fall of the Great Powers*, (NY: Random House, 1987)

3   "America has spent $5.9 trillion on wars in the Middle East and Asia since 2001, a new study says," *CNBC*, November 14, 2018, https://www.cnbc.com/2018/11/14/us-has-spent-5point9-trillion-on-middle-east-asia-wars-since-2001-study.html

4   Evan Feigenbaum, "Reluctant Stakeholder: Why China's Highly Strategic Brand of Revisionism is More Challenging Than Washington Thinks," *Carnegie Endowment*, April 27, 2018, https://carnegieendowment.org/2018/04/27/reluctant-stakeholder-why-china-s-highly-strategic-brand-of-revisionism-is-more-challenging-than-washington-thinks-pub-76213

5   U.S. Treasury Department presentation, https://www.treasury.gov/resource-center/data-chart-center/quarterly-refunding/Documents/q12019CombinedChargesforArchives.pdf

6   Camilo E. Tovar and Tania Mohd Nor, Reserve Currency Blocs: A Changing International Monetary System?, IMF Working Paper, January 2018, https://www.imf.org/~/media/Files/Publications/WP/2018/wp1820.ashx

7   Barry Eichengreen, *Exorbitant Privilege*.

8   Retooling Global Development, World Economic and Social Survey 2010, United Nations, Department of Economic and Social Affairs, 2010.

9   Enhancing International Monetary Stability—A Role for the SDR?, International Monetary Fund, January 7, 2011, https://www.imf.org/external/np/pp/eng/2011/010711.pdf

10  "Russian President Vladimir Putin says US dominance is ending after mistakes 'typical of an empire'," *ABC News*, October 19, 2018, https://abcnews.go.com/International/putin-us-dominance-ending-mistakes-typical-empire/story?id=58611354

11  "Niall Ferguson: The US Has 6 Years Before Debt Payments Surpass Defense Spending," *Business Insider*, July 6, 2010,

https://www.businessinsider.com/niall-ferguson-the-us-has-6-years-before-debt-payments-surpass-defense-spending-2010-7

12  "US could spend more on servicing debt than defense by 2024: study," *The Hill*, March 15, 2018, https://thehill.com/policy/finance/378607-us-could-spend-more-on-servicing-debt-than-defense-by-2024-study

13  "U.S. on a Course to Spend More on Debt than Defense," *Wall Street Journal*, November 11, 2018, https://www.wsj.com/articles/u-s-on-a-course-to-spend-more-on-debt-than-defense-1541937600

14  U.S. Treasury Department presentation, https://www.treasury.gov/resource-center/data-chart-center/quarterly-refunding/Documents/q12019CombinedChargesforArchives.pdf

## Chapter 1. Weaponizing Currency

1  "Iran Deal Advocate Says EU Will Have to Bend to U.S. Sanctions," *Bloomberg*, September 12, 2018, https://www.bloomberg.com/news/articles/2018-09-12/iran-deal-advocate-says-eu-will-have-to-bend-to-u-s-sanctions

2  Woodrow Wilson, quoted in Gary Clyde Hufbauer, Jeffrey J. Schott, Kimberly Ann Elliott, and Barbara Oegg, *Economic Sanctions Reconsidered*, Peterson Institute for International Economics, 2009, p. 9.

3  https://www.treasury.gov/ofac/downloads/sdnlist.pdf

4  Gibson Dunn, 2017 Year-end sanctions update, February 5, 2018, https://www.gibsondunn.com/wp-content/uploads/2018/02/2017-year-end-sanctions-update.pdf

5  Countering America's Adversaries through Sanctions Act, https://www.treasury.gov/resource-center/sanctions/Programs/Documents/hr3364_pl115-44.pdf

6   "US imposes sanctions against Russian oligarchs and government officials," *CNN*, April 6, 2018, https://edition.cnn.com/2018/04/06/politics/russia-sanctions-oligarchs/index.html

7   "Why expat Americans are giving up their passports," *BBC*, February 9, 2016, https://www.bbc.com/news/35383435

8   Interview with Henry Kissinger, *Spiegel*, November 13, 2014, http://www.spiegel.de/international/world/interview-with-henry-kissinger-on-state-of-global-politics-a-1002073.html

9   See for example Peter Harrell, "Is the U.S. Using Sanctions Too Aggressively?," *Foreign Affairs*, September 11, 2018, https://www.foreignaffairs.com/articles/2018-09-11/us-using-sanctions-too-aggressively and Jacob Lew and Richard Nephew, "The Use and Misuse of Economic Statecraft," *Foreign Affairs*, November/December 2018, https://www.foreignaffairs.com/articles/world/2018-10-15/use-and-misuse-economic-statecraft

10  "Lew Defends Sanctions, but Cautions on Overuse," *New York Times, March 29, 2016,* https://www.nytimes.com/2016/03/30/us/politics/lew-defends-sanctions-but-cautions-on-overuse.html

11  "Banning Russian banks is act of war: Putin ally warns global elite after threat of sanctions," *Daily Mail*, January 28, 2018, https://www.thisismoney.co.uk/money/news/article-5303763/Banning-Russian-banks-act-war-says-Putin-ally.html

12  "Treasury's Mnuchin: China may face new sanctions on North Korea," *Reuters*, September 12, 2017, https://www.reuters.com/article/us-northkorea-sanctions-treasury/treasurys-mnuchin-china-may-face-new-sanctions-on-north-korea-idUSKCN1BN1P1

13  "Wir lassen nicht zu, dass die USA über unsere Köpfe hinweg handeln," *Handelsblatt*, August 21, 2018, https://www.handelsblatt.com/meinung/gastbeitraege/gastkommentar-wir-lassen-nicht-zu-dass-die-usa-ueber-unsere-koepfe-hinweg-handeln/22933006.html

14 "Russian banks join Chinese alternative payment system," *RT*, March 30, 2019, https://www.rt.com/business/455121-russian-banks-chinese-swift/

15 Interview with Henry Kissinger, *Spiegel*, November 13, 2014, http://www.spiegel.de/international/world/interview-with-henry-kissinger-on-state-of-global-politics-a-1002073.html

## Chapter 2. The dollar busters

1 "China, Russia urged to continue efforts to defang US-dollar sanctions weapon," *South China Morning Press*, June 6, 2019, https://www.scmp.com/economy/global-economy/article/3013246/china-russia-urged-continue-efforts-defang-us-dollar

2 "Russia seeks to dump dollar as new US sanctions loom," *The Bull*, November 7, 2018, https://thebull.com.au/78200-russia-seeks-to-dump-dollar-as-new-us-sanctions-loom/

3 "Russia wants to get rid of the domination of the dollar," *Lenta*, February 9, 2018, https://lenta.ru/news/2018/02/09/kostin/

4 "Russian gold reserves top $100 billion after adding another 600,000 ounces to its vast stockpile," *RT*, July 25, 2019, https://www.rt.com/business/465054-russian-gold-reserves-100-billion/

5 "Russia shifts $100bn of its reserves into yuan, yen & euro in a great dollar dump," *RT*, January 10, 2019, https://www.rt.com/business/448441-russia-reserves-dollar-dump/

6 "Sergey Glazyev on the Dollar Monopoly and the War," *TASS*, April 26, 2017, http://www.defenddemocracy.press/sergey-glazyev-on-the-dollar-monopoly-and-the-war/

7 "Iranian FM: We have 'perfected the art of evading sanctions'," *Times of Israel*, December 15, 2018, https://www.timesofisrael.com/iranian-fm-we-have-perfected-the-art-of-evading-sanctions/

8 "Iran switches from dollar to euro for official reporting currency, *Reuters*, April 18, 2018, https://www.reuters.com/article/

9   us-iran-currency-euro/iran-switches-from-dollar-to-euro-for-official-reporting-currency-idUSKBN1HP25W
    "Iran's Zarif calls for elimination dollar to stop US economic terrorism," *Sputnik*, June 9, 2019, https://sputniknews.com/world/201906091075756703-irans-zarif-calls-elimination-dollar-stop-us-economic-terrorism/

10  "Sarkozy Brings Message on Dollar to U.S.," *New York Times*, January 11, 2011, https://www.nytimes.com/2011/01/11/world/europe/11iht-france11.html

11  "Issue of Sovereignty: Macron wants the EU to be less dependent on the dollar," *Sputnik News*, November 12, 2018, https://sputniknews.com/europe/201811121069726271-macron-less-dependent-eu-dollar/

12  "EU's Tusk asks: 'With friends like Trump, who needs enemies?'," *Reuters*, May 16, 2018, https://www.reuters.com/article/us-usa-trump-eu/eus-tusk-asks-with-friends-like-trump-who-needs-enemies-idUSKCN1IH1OH

13  "EU Looking to Sidestep U.S. Sanctions With Payments System Plan," *Bloomberg*, August 27, 2018, https://www.bloomberg.com/news/articles/2018-08-27/eu-looking-to-sidestep-u-s-sanctions-with-payments-system-plan

14  Remarks by High Representative/Vice-President Federica Mogherini following a Ministerial Meeting of E3/EU + 2 and Iran, September 24, 2018, https://eeas.europa.eu/headquarters/headquarters-homepage/51040/remarks-hrvp-mogherini-following-ministerial-meeting-e3eu-2-and-iran_en

15  Statement by High Representative/Vice-President Federica Mogherini on the creation of INSTEX, Instrument for Supporting Trade Exchanges, January 31, 2019, https://eeas.europa.eu/headquarters/headquarters-homepage/57475/statement-high-representativevice-president-federica-mogherini-creation-instex-instrument_en

16 "Brussels sets out plan for euro to challenge dollar dominance," *Financial Times*, December 3, 2018, https://www.ft.com/content/58927e22-f729-11e8-af46-2022a0b02a6c

17 Operation dollar dump: can Turkey rely on the lira in international trade?, *Sputnik*, August, 11, 2018, https://sputniknews.com/analysis/201808111067120197-turkey-us-de-dollarization-brics/

18 "Turkey to become 5th largest economy in the world by 2030, Standard Chartered predicts," *Daily Sabah*, January 9, 2019, https://www.dailysabah.com/economy/2019/01/09/turkey-to-become-5th-largest-economy-in-the-world-by-2030-standard-chartered-predicts

19 "Chavez backs dropping U.S. dollar for oil trade," *Reuters*, October 17, 2009, https://www.reuters.com/article/venezuela-opec/chavez-backs-dropping-u-s-dollar-for-oil-trade-idUSN1731520620091017

20 "Dollars Are Out, Euros Are In as U.S. Sanctions Sting Venezuela," *Bloomberg*, October 16, 2018, https://www.bloomberg.com/news/articles/2018-10-16/dollars-are-out-euros-are-in-as-u-s-sanctions-sting-venezuela

21 "Exclusive: Russia Secretly Helped Venezuela Launch a Cryptocurrency to Evade U.S. Sanctions," *Time Magazine*, March 20, 2018, http://time.com/5206835/exclusive-russia-petro-venezuela-cryptocurrency/ and "In Venezuela, Russia pockets key energy assets in exchange for cash bailouts," *Washington Post*, December 24, 2018, https://www.washingtonpost.com/world/national-security/in-venezuela-russia-pockets-key-energy-assets-in-exchange-for-cash-bailouts/2018/12/20/da458db6-f403-11e8-80d0-f7e1948d55f4_story.html

22 "Air pollution in India caused 1.2 million deaths last year," *Quartz*, December 8, 2018, https://qz.com/1489086/air-pollution-in-india-caused-1-2-million-deaths-last-year/

23 "India & Iran drop dollar in oil trade to bypass US sanctions—report," RT, May 30, 2018, https://www.rt.com/business/428245-india-iran-dollar-rupee-oil/

24 "India, Russia see to skirt US sanctions threat to arms deals," Bloomberg, July 15, 2019, https://www.bloomberg.com/news/articles/2019-07-15/india-russia-seek-to-skirt-u-s-sanctions-threat-to-arms-deals

25 "China, Pakistan Agree to Conduct Bilateral Trade in Yuan," Voice of America, November 5, 2018, https://www.voanews.com/a/china-pakistan-agree-to-conduct-bilateral-trade-in-yuan/4645164.html

## Chapter 3. Is red the new green

1 "Trump labels China a strategic competitor," *Financial Times*, December 19, 2017, https://www.ft.com/content/215cf8fa-e3cb-11e7-8b99-0191e45377ec

2 "Oil for security fueled close ties," *Washington Post*, February 11, 2002, https://www.washingtonpost.com/archive/politics/2002/02/11/oil-for-security-fueled-close-ties/fdf1f123-214f-41b3-a53c-a5e687c648e7

3 Quoted from Vaclav Smil, *Making the Modern World: Materials and Dematerialization*, in Bill Gates' blog, June 12, 2014, https://www.gatesnotes.com/Books/Making-the-Modern-World

4 Larry Summers, "Time US Leadership Woke Up to New Economic Era," Larry Summers (blog), April 5, 2015, http://larrysummers.com/2015/04/05/time-us-leadership-woke-up-to-new-economic-era/.

5 "US warms up to 'Belt and Road' business potential," *South China Morning Press*, May 14, 2017, https://www.scmp.com/news/china/diplomacy-defence/article/2094295/us-warms-belt-and-road-business-potential

6 "United States says it supports China's infrastructure connectivity plan," *Reuters*, May 14, 2017, https://www.reuters.com/article/us-china-silkroad-usa/united-states-says-it-supports-chinas-infrastructure-connectivity-plan-idUSKCN18A0D2

7 Mike Pence to unveil rival to 'dangerous' Belt and Road Initiative at APEC Summit, *South China Morning Press*, November 15, 2018, https://www.scmp.com/week-asia/geopolitics/article/2173326/mike-pence-unveil-rival-dangerous-belt-and-road-initiative

8 "China opens up about its forex reserves," *Caixin Daily*, July 30, 2019, https://mailchi.mp/caixin/cx-daily-us-and-china-finally-resume-trade-talks-268363

9 "Mnuchin: Not worried about China selling Treasuries, 'lot of buyers' for US debt," *CNBC*, April 6, 2018, https://www.cnbc.com/2018/04/06/mnuchin-not-worried-about-china-selling-treasurys-lot-of-buyers-for-us-debt.html

10 "Exclusive: China not seriously considering U.S. Treasuries as trade war weapon—envoy," *Reuters*, November 27, 2018, https://www.reuters.com/article/us-usa-trade-china-treasuries-exclusive/exclusive-china-not-seriously-considering-us-treasuries-as-trade-war-weapon-envoy-idUSKCN1NW2HF

11 *The Budget and Economic Outlook 2018-2028*, Congressional Budget Office, April 2018, https://www.cbo.gov/system/files?file=115th-congress-2017-2018/reports/53651-outlook.pdf

12 "The China Story that is far bigger than Apple," *Wall Street Journal*, January 4, 2019, https://www.wsj.com/articles/the-china-story-that-is-far-bigger-than-apple-11546598005

13 "China Is Buying More and More Gold as the Trade War Drags On," *Bloomberg*, June 10, 2019, https://www.bloomberg.com/news/articles/2019-06-10/china-snaps-up-more-gold-in-six-month-spree-as-tensions-escalate

14 "China calls for a new reserve currency," *Financial Times*, March 23, 2009, https://www.ft.com/content/7851925a-17a2-11de-8c9d-0000779fd2ac

15 "ECB completes foreign reserves investment in Chinese renminbi equivalent to €500 million," European Central Bank Press Release, June 13, 2017, https://www.ecb.europa.eu/press/pr/date/2017/html/ecb.pr170613.en.html

16 Currency Composition of Official Foreign Exchange Reserves, IMF, http://data.imf.org/?sk=E6A5F467-C14B-4AA8-9F6D-5A09EC4E62A4

17 "The Dollar Underpins American Power. Rivals Are Building Workarounds," *Wall Street Journal*, May 29, 2019, https://www.wsj.com/articles/the-dollar-powers-american-dominance-rivals-are-building-workarounds-11559155440

18 "Africa: Dedollarization on the rise," *Financial Times*, September 17, 2017, https://www.ft.com/content/f9933eb0-fbac-361c-8427-36b60a42b9fa

19 "Kenya mulls adoption of Chinese yuan as a reserve currency," *New China*, June 13, 2018, http://www.xinhuanet.com/english/2018-06/13/c_137249686.htm

20 "Interview: African economy needs more usage of Chinese yuan: financial expert," *New China*, June 2, 2018, http://www.xinhuanet.com/english/2018-06/02/c_137225509.htm

21 "Philippines, China launch peso-yuan trading facility," *Rapler*, October 30, 2018, https://www.rappler.com/business/215587-philippines-china-launch-peso-yuan-trading-facility

22 "China lobbies ASEAN on yuan use, cracking dollar dominance," *Nikkei, April 26, 2019*, https://asia.nikkei.com/Business/Markets/Currencies/China-lobbies-ASEAN-on-yuan-use-cracking-dollar-dominance

23 https://www.cgdev.org/sites/default/files/examining-debt-implications-belt-and-road-initiative-policy-perspective.pdf

## Chapter 4. As good as gold: From Petrodollar to Petroyuan

1. "EU chief aims to boost euro's role in world market," *AP News*, September 12, 2018, https://www.apnews.com/fa72ac5836414cd2985988feec6fcfad
2. Gal Luft and Anne Korin, *Turning Oil into Salt: Energy Security through Fuel Choice*, 2010.
3. "The international role of the euro: down but not out," Speech by Claudio Borio Head of the Monetary and Economic Department, Bank of International Settlements, April 9, 2019, https://www.bis.org/speeches/sp190404.pdf
4. Speech by Richard Nixon, August 15, 1971, https://www.cvce.eu/content/publication/1999/1/1/168eed17-f28b-487b-9cd2-6d668e42e63a/publishable_en.pdf
5. "President Trump Says U.S. Would Be 'Foolish' to Cancel Saudi Arms Deals," *Time Magazine*, October 13, 2018, http://time.com/5424150/trump-saudi-arabia-arms-deal/
6. "China will 'compel' Saudi Arabia to trade oil in yuan — and that's going to affect the US dollar," *CNBC*, October 11, 2017, https://www.cnbc.com/2017/10/11/china-will-compel-saudi-arabia-to-trade-oil-in-yuan--and-thats-going-to-affect-the-us-dollar.html
7. "Saudi Arabia Warns of Economic Fallout if Congress Passes 9/11 Bill," *New York Times, April 15, 2016,* https://www.nytimes.com/2016/04/16/world/middleeast/saudi-arabia-warns-ofeconomic-fallout-if-congress-passes-9-11-bill.html
8. "Exclusive Saudi Arabia threatens to ditch dollar oil trades to stop NOPEC sources," *Reuters*, April 5, 2019, https://www.reuters.com/article/us-saudi-usa-oil-exclusive/exclusive-saudi-arabia-threatens-to-ditch-dollar-oil-trades-to-stop-nopec-sources-idUSKCN1RH008
9. "China to open up access to yuan-denominated commodity futures contracts as trade war escalates," *South China Morning Press*, May 28,

2019, https://www.scmp.com/business/china-business/article/3012161/china-open-access-yuan-denominated-commodity-futures

10. "Analysis: China's flawed futures contract pushes oil trade to record high in 2018," *Reuters*, December 12, 2018, https://in.reuters.com/article/crude-oil-futures-china/analysis-chinas-flawed-futures-contract-pushes-oil-trade-to-record-high-in-2018-idINKBN1OB16D

11. John van Schaik, "How Governments Sell Their Oil?," Revenue Watch Institute, April 2012, https://resourcegovernance.org/sites/default/files/OilSales-HowGovtsSellOil.pdf

## Chapter 5. Another BRICS in the wall

1. "Putin and Xi cement an alliance for the 21$^{st}$ century," *Washington Post*, June 6, 2019, https://www.washingtonpost.com/world/2019/06/06/putin-xi-cement-st-century-alliance

2. "Russia, China to sign agreement on payments in national currencies, says decree," *TASS*, June 5, 2019, http://tass.com/economy/1061848

3. National Security Strategy, The White House, December 2017, https://www.whitehouse.gov/wp-content/uploads/2017/12/NSS-Final-12-18-2017-0905.pdf

4. 2018 National Defense Strategy of the United States of America, U.S. Department of Defense, https://dod.defense.gov/Portals/1/Documents/pubs/2018-National-Defense-Strategy-Summary.pdf

5. "U.S. intel agencies: Russia and China plotting to interfere in 2020 election," *NBC News*, January 29, 2019, https://www.nbcnews.com/politics/national-security/u-s-intel-agencies-russia-china-plotting-interfere-2020-election-n963896

6     Adam Zwass, *The Council for Mutual Economic Assistance: The Thorny Path from Political Integration,* (NY and London: M.E. Sharpie, 1989), p. 78.

7     "Erdoğan suggests adding 'T' to BRICS," *Hurriyet Daily News*, July 29, 2018, http://www.hurriyetdailynews.com/erdogan-suggests-adding-t-to-brics-135160

8     "Egypt hails BRICS plus initiative," *Africa News*, September 2, 2017, https://www.africanews.com/2017/09/02/egypt-hails-brics-plus-initiative

9     "Malaysia's Mahathir Mohamed goes for gold," *Forbes*, June 3, 2019, https://www.forbes.com/sites/stevehanke/2019/06/03/malaysias-mahathir-mohamed-goes-for-gold

10     "China builds up gold reserves in shift away from dollar," *Nikkei*, January 24, 2019, https://asia.nikkei.com/Business/Markets/Commodities/China-builds-up-gold-reserves-in-shift-away-from-dollar

11     See for example Koos Jensen "PBOC gold purchases: separating facts from speculation," *Bullion Star*, July 20, 2017, https://www.bullionstar.com/blogs/koos-jansen/pboc-gold-purchases-separating-facts-from-speculation/ and Dominic Frisby, "How much gold does China have? A lot more than you think," *Money Week*, December 12, 2018, https://moneyweek.com/499249/how-much-gold-does-china-have-a-lot-more-than-you-think/ and "Skepticism reigns about the true state of the Chinese Central Bank gold reserves," *Bullion Star,* October 12, 2018, https://www.bullionstar.com/blogs/ronan-manly/skepticism-reigns-true-state-chinese-central-bank-gold-reserves/

12     James Rickards, *The Death of Money: The Coming Collapse of the International Monetary System,* (New York, Portfolio Penguin, 2014), p. 229.

## Chapter 6. Rising Phoenix

1. "Get ready for the Phoenix," *Economist*, September 1, 1988.
2. "Global Debt of $244 Trillion Nears Record Despite Faster Growth," *Bloomberg*, January 15, 2019, https://www.bloomberg.com/news/articles/2019-01-15/global-debt-of-244-trillion-nears-record-despite-faster-growth
3. "Bitcoin is the 'mother of all scams' and Blockchain is most hyped tech ever, Roubini tells Congress," *CNBC*, October 11, 2018, https://www.cnbc.com/2018/10/11/roubini-bitcoin-is-mother-of-all-scams.html
4. Erik Townsend, *Beyond Blockchain: The Death of the Dollar and the Rise of Digital Currency*, (Amazon Digital Services, 2018).
5. Record high remittances sent globally in 2018, World Bank Press Release, April 8, 2019, https://www.worldbank.org/en/news/press-release/2019/04/08/record-high-remittances-sent-globally-in-2018
6. NBC/Wall Street Journal survey, March 2019, https://www.documentcloud.org/documents/5794861-19093-NBCWSJ-March-Poll-4-5-19-Release.html
7. "The arrogance and genius of Libra coin," *The Medium*, June 25, 2019, https://medium.com/s/no-mercy-no-malice/profg-coin-scorpio-7d386a96dc65
8. "Central bank unveils plan on digital currency," *China Daily*, July 9, 2019, http://www.chinadaily.com.cn/a/201907/09/WS5d239217a3105895c2e7c56f.html
9. "China's Central Bank Seeks Digital Currency Specialists," Coin 360, October 11, 2018, https://cointelegraph.com/news/chinas-central-bank-seeks-digital-currency-specialists
10. "People's Bank of China Considers Supporting Yuan-Pegged Stablecoin Tokens," *Bitcoin Exchange Guide*, October 10, 2018, https://bitcoinexchangeguide.com/peoples-bank-of-china-considers-supporting-yuan-pegged-stablecoin-tokens/

11  "Why millennials are driving cashless revolution in China," *Financial Times*, July 17, 2018, https://www.ft.com/content/539e39b8-851b-11e8-a29d-73e3d454535d

## Chapter 7. Alice in Wonderland economics

1  "Global Debt of $244 Trillion Nears Record Despite Faster Growth," *Bloomberg*, January 15, 2019, https://www.bloomberg.com/news/articles/2019-01-15/global-debt-of-244-trillion-nears-record-despite-faster-growth also "New Data on Global Debt," *IMF Blog*, January 2, 2019, https://blogs.imf.org/2019/01/02/new-data-on-global-debt/

2  For up to date statistics on U.S. debts and liabilities visit https://www.usdebtclock.org

3  "As Debt Rises, the Government Will Soon Spend More on Interest Than on the Military," *New York Times*, September 25, 2018, https://www.nytimes.com/2018/09/25/business/economy/us-government-debt-interest.html

4  Statistical release: OTC derivatives statistics at end June 2018, Bank of International Settlements, October 31, 2018, https://www.bis.org/publ/otc_hy1810.pdf

5  Berkshire Hathaway 2002 letter to investors, http://www.berkshirehathaway.com/letters/2002pdf.pdf

6  "Kudlow: Fed may not hike interest rates 'in my lifetime'," *Politico*, April 11, 2019, https://www.politico.com/story/2019/04/11/larry-kudlow-interest-rates-1269762

7  U.S. Treasury Department presentation, https://www.treasury.gov/resource-center/data-chart-center/quarterly-refunding/Documents/q12019CombinedChargesforArchives.pdf

8  "How America Learned to Stop Worrying and Love Deficits and Debt," *New York Times*, February 23, 2019, https://www.nytimes.com/2019/02/23/upshot/how-america-learned-to-stop-worrying-and-love-deficits-and-debt.html

9. "Warren Buffett argues government budget deficits don't matter," *Axios*, February 24, 2019, https://www.axios.com/warren-buffett-national-debt-6fa22c24-bc40-4cda-8895-973605ea465a.html

10. Jason Furman and Lawrence H. Summers, "Who is Afraid of Budget Deficits," *Foreign Affairs*, January 29, 2019, https://www.foreignaffairs.com/articles/2019-01-27/whos-afraid-budget-deficits?

11. Stephanie Kelton, Andres Bernal, and Greg Carlock, "We Can Pay For a Green New Deal," *Huffington Post*, November 30, 2018, https://www.huffingtonpost.com/entry/opinion-green-new-deal-cost_us_5c0042b2e4b027f1097bda5b

12. "Modern Monetary Theory explained by Stephanie Kelton," *CNBC*, March 4, 2019, https://www.cnbc.com/video/2019/03/01/stephanie-kelton-explains-modern-monetary-theory.html

13. "Explainer: What is Modern Monetary Theory," *The Conversation*, January 31, 2017, https://theconversation.com/explainer-what-is-modern-monetary-theory-72095

14. "Modern Monetary Theory explained by Stephanie Kelton," *CNBC*, March 4, 2019, https://www.cnbc.com/video/2019/03/01/stephanie-kelton-explains-modern-monetary-theory.html

15. Ibid

16. Donald Trump tweet, May 22, 2019, https://twitter.com/realdonaldtrump/status/1131243666968911875

17. Graham Allison, *Destined for War: Can America and China Escape Thucydides's Trap?*, (NY: Houghton Mifflin Harcourt; Reprint edition 2017)

18. "Imagining the dollar without its privilege," *New York times*, October 15, 2013, https://www.nytimes.com/2013/10/16/business/imagining-the-dollar-without-its-privilege.html

## Chapter 8. Toward a currency protection strategy

1. Donald Trump tweet, February 21, 2019, https://twitter.com/realdonaldtrump/status/1098583029713420288
2. "The Fourth Industrial Revolution by Klaus Schwab," World Economic Forum, https://www.weforum.org/about/the-fourth-industrial-revolution-by-klaus-schwab
3. "Greenspan warns U.S. budget deficit will ultimately lead to higher inflation," *Market Watch, March 1, 2019,* https://www.marketwatch.com/story/greenspan-warns-us-budget-deficit-will-ultimately-lead-to-higher-inflation-2019-02-28
4. "Fed Chairman Powell says he is 'very worried' about growing amount of US debt," *CNBC,* January 10, 2019, https://www.cnbc.com/2019/01/10/fed-chairman-powell-says-he-is-very-worried-about-growing-amount-of-us-debt.html
5. "Trump says Federal Reserve policies are 'very destructive' to U.S. economy," *CBS News,* June 10, 2019, https://www.cbsnews.com/news/donald-trump-federal-reserve-policies-are-very-destructive-to-us-economy/
6. For more detailed recommendations see Gal Luft, *Silk Road 2.0: US Strategy toward China's Belt and Road Initiative*, Atlantic Council, October 2017, https://www.atlanticcouncil.org/images/US_Strategy_toward_Chinas_BRI_web_1003.pdf
7. JP Morgan is rolling out the first US bank-backed cryptocurrency to transform payments business, *CNBC,* February 14, 2019, https://www.cnbc.com/2019/02/13/jp-morgan-is-rolling-out-the-first-us-bank-backed-cryptocurrency-to-transform-payments--.html

## Epilogue

1. U.S. Treasury Department presentation, https://www.treasury.gov/resource-center/data-chart-center/quarterly-refunding/Documents/q12019CombinedChargesforArchives.pdf

www.ingramcontent.com/pod-product-compliance
Lightning Source LLC
Chambersburg PA
CBHW070624220526
45466CB00001B/94